Against

Multiple Myeloma

A true story by the cancer survivor

A real case study on multiple myeloma
How to use immune system to fight cancer?
How to use nature's gift to fight cancer?
How to live in harmony with nature?
Must read for all

C K Sreedharan

Contents

This book is dedicated

to

my wonderful wife **Shanthi**

and

to

my loving daughters

Saranya and **Suchitra**

Foreword

True stories generally exaggerate and try to present a larger than life story. But this true story- 'Battle against Multiple Myeloma- A true story by the cancer survivor,' is an exception.

As an oncologist, practicing for decades, I have treated innumerable cases of various types of cancer. I am deeply disturbed to see the increase in the number of patients who are detected for cancer. In my experience I have seen the very mention of the word 'cancer' making people despondent and giving up all hopes of survival. Cancer is no doubt a deadly disease, but I would like to stress here that like any other disease it can also be treated, if detected early.

CK Sreedharan, whom I treated and continue to provide medical advice for multiple myeloma, has brought out vividly the trauma and the practical difficulties that are suffered by the cancer patients. The author has lucidly explained his cancer experience from detection to treatment, supported by actual medical test reports, in a style that is easy to understand. His fighting spirit, determination and tenacity in battling the disease are commendable. This is a motivating and a strong positive message for the cancer patients and the cancer survivors.

I am optimistic by reading this book every victim of cancer is inspired and is determined to fight for survival under every possible trying circumstance. I look forward to survivors like CK Sreedharan to share their experiences with the world, in order to remove the fear and the hopelessness associated with the disorder.

It is a pleasure to write foreword for this book of personal experience. I sincerely hope that not only the cancer victims, but also others to derive maximum benefit out of this book.

Dr. Sachin V Almel,
M D, D M (ONCO),
Consultant Medical Oncologist,
P D Hinduja National Hospital & Medical Centre,
Veer Savarkar Marg, Mahim, Mumbai- 400016, India.

Acknowledgement

It is not the intention of the author to recommend a particular doctor, or a hospital or any particular form of treatment. The entire book is based on the experience of the author. The suggestions are also for information purpose only. It is strongly and emphatically advised to discuss the particular case at all times with the treating doctor / oncologist, as the case may be.

Caner is not a new subject and I am not the first one to write about it. Several eminent experts in the field have already written well researched books on this topic. I have liberally made use of the ideas, information and explanations from several published sources which are in public domain and I am indebted to all the distinguished authors, writers and contributors. All though every possible care is taken to acknowledge every source of information, some may have been inadvertently missed out. In such an eventuality, the lapse may be ignored and the author may be kindly excused.

The author has used his own original scanned copies of various tests and investigations for authenticity and to facilitate real experience sharing. These shall not be used or quoted under any circumstance without the permission of the author in writing.

Part of the royalty earned through the sale proceeds of this book will be donated to 'Cancer Fund' of National Health & Education Society, Veer Savarkar Marg, Mahim, Mumbai-400016, India, as a tribute to the charitable services undertaken by the society to support the needy and the downtrodden cancer patients. It is a registered society under the Bombay Public Trust Act and manages the P D Hinduja National Hospital, Mahim, Mumbai, India.

Prologue

'When we tackle obstacles, we find hidden reserves of courage and resilience we did not know we had. And then we realize that these resources were always there within us.'
- APJ Abdul Kalam.

I was diagnosed with multiple myeloma, a type of blood cancer in April 2008. I underwent treatment at P D Hinduja National Hospital, Mahim, Mumbai, India. Dr. Sachin Almel, MD – one of the leading oncologists of the country treated me. I still continue to consult him once in every year, which I will continue till my life time. In fact I am really pained to see the number of patients seeking treatment for multiple myeloma increasing at alarming proportions from the time I underwent the treatment. I admire Dr. Sachin Almel for his efficiency and expertise in dealing with the patients. Due to this dedication to the profession, he is able to provide medical advice to ever increasing number of patients every day. Dr. Sachin and I share mutual respect. We have also developed good rapport and admiration for each other over the period of time.

One more young girl by name Priyanka (name changed to protect identity), also underwent treatment for multiple myeloma during my treatment period. Her case is also more or less similar to my case.

She was not aware of the extent of damage done by the disease to her spinal cord till the time the disease was actually diagnosed. One day she was riding pillion on a motor cycle, along with her friend in Pune. The bike climbed over a steep speed breaker, which resulted in considerable jerk to the body of Priyanka. The girl felt severe pain in her spinal cord and she was immediately rushed to the hospital. After a thorough medical examination, it was diagnosed that some links in her spinal cord had collapsed due to compression fracture. The reason for the fracture was not the speed breaker, but the disease multiple myeloma, which eroded her bone over a period of time, without the knowledge of the victim. Priyanka had to undergo spinal cord reconstruction at some portions, a delicate, critical and an expensive medical procedure followed by chemotherapy and stem-cell treatment.

Normally it is claimed that multiple myeloma affects people above 50 years of age. But it is not true. The disease can manifest at any age. Priyanka is an example; she was just 20 years when she was diagnosed with multiple myeloma.

After my case, Dr. Sachin Almel started referring patients diagnosed with multiple myeloma to speak to me to know about my personal experience and also to get convinced about the effectiveness of the stem-cell treatment procedure, which is one of the standard treatment procedures followed world-wide. I also counselled several multiple myeloma patients regarding the efficacy and the effectiveness of stem-cell treatment procedure. I have shared my experience with the patients, encouraged and tried to remove their fear and anxiety.

On November 19, 2016 I received a call from an unknown number and I answered the call. The conversation went something like below:

'Am I speaking to Mr. Sreedharan?' an unknown lady asked me.

'You are right. Sreedharan here,' I answered.

'Your number was given by Dr. Sachin Almel of Hinduja Hospital,' the caller said.

Immediately I realized that it was a counselling call.

'What can I do for you madam?' I asked the anxious caller.

'Sir, Dr. Sachin told us that you had successfully undergone stem-cell treatment under him. Will you please tell us about your experience?' the lady pleaded.

'Are you the patient?' I asked.

'No. It is my mother. She is undergoing treatment for multiple myeloma under Dr. Almel. She has completed four cycles of chemotherapy session. The doctor has further advised to go for stem-cell therapy to prolong the remission period of the disease,' the woman replied.

'How old is your mother?' I further enquired.

'She is 55 years old. We are all concerned about the stem-cell treatment.'

'Madam, there is nothing to worry. I also underwent the same treatment when I was 50 years old. It is more than eight years now. Till now I have no problem and I am in good health. All my yearly follow-up check-up medical reports are normal,' I said with conviction.

'Dr. Sachin discussed your case with us and also explained the complete procedure. Still we would like to hear from you Sir,' again pleaded the woman.

'Do not worry. The procedure is simple. The attending doctor decides the number of chemotherapy cycles the patient has to undergo depending on the condition of the patient and the extent of spread of the disease. The chemotherapy cycles may vary from four to six cycles. The patient may be advised to undergo stem cell treatment immediately after the completion of chemotherapy cycles,' I explained in brief.

'My mother's chemotherapy cycles are over. We have to decide now about the stem cell treatment. Is the treatment safe for my aged mother?'

'It is a safe and a simple procedure. Patient's own stem cells (called as autologous stem cells) are extracted from patient's blood through a computer monitored process. The patient is given a high dosage of chemotherapy, to destroy all the existing blood cells. After this complete destruction, the previously collected stem cells are intravenously reintroduced into the body. The stem cells slowly and gradually rebuild fresh blood cells.' I explained the procedure in a simple way.

'Can the treatment be better and more effective if taken abroad, say UK or USA?' the lady asked.

I realized that the patient must be rich and from a wealthy family. I wanted to strongly demolish the myth.

'I would definitely advice not to go abroad for the treatment. The reason being the stem cell treatment is standardized all over the world. All the reputed hospitals across the globe follow the same standardized procedure. The patient gets the same treatment everywhere. From my personal experience I can categorically say that the treatment given at Hinduja is also at par with other hospitals in the advanced countries. Same treatment in abroad may cost you many times more than what you pay here. Presently you can see many foreigners flocking to Indian hospitals for cancer treatment due to the quality of treatment and the reasonable cost of treatment. You can be rest assured that Hinduja hospital and the panel of doctors in the hospital are at par with the best in the world,' I emphatically tried to reassure the lady.

'Sir, will you please tell us, what are the precautions the patient has to follow?' asked the lady, seemed to be apparently convinced with my explanation.

'Madam, Dr. Sachin Almel is one of the best oncologists in the country and he is at Hinduja. The patient will be under the care of an expert doctor assisted by an experienced and competent nursing team. Have complete faith in the doctor and simply follow his instructions. The patient will make remarkable progress,' the conversation ended.

The lady seemed to be satisfied now. She thanked me profusely for sharing my experience with her.

During the last eight years Dr. Sachin Almel referred several patients to talk to me to know about my experience and to get convinced in the treatment. I received several distressed calls and each time I counselled sharing my real experience, without any exaggeration. I have become a symbol of hope and confidence builder for the diseased and the mentally distressed patients. By sharing my experience with the patients of multiple myeloma, I try to bring in a little comfort and solace to the sufferers.

This is the first motivating factor which inspired me to share my experience with the patients of multiple myeloma through the book, so that I can create a ray of hope and confidence in the victims of the dreaded disease.

I am ashamed to admit that till the time I was diagnosed with the disease, for almost fifty years of my life time, I had not done any charity .During my engineering college days, I was a group leader of National Service Scheme (NSS). As a volunteer of NSS, my charitable act towards the community was just limited to donation of blood on a few occasions. During my course of treatment, soon after my stem cell transplant, many unknown strangers and unrelated kind hearted people voluntarily lined up to donate platelets. There were quite a few great souls who quietly came, donated platelets, silently left without revealing their identity. I really can't find any suitable word to express my gratitude to all those unknown donors. Existence of such generous and humble human beings in the present commercial world really strengthens one's belief in the existence of the Universal Power or the God Almighty.

When I look back and brood over the past, I am really overwhelmed by the support- moral, physical, financial and the helping hand extended by so many known and unknown people. There were several firms and individuals who extended financial support. After undergoing the treatment I realized that cancer the disease, is not the real killer. But the associated treatment costs, the mental agony and the distress the patient and his / her close relatives undergo are the main culprits which actually kill the patient and destroy the family.

More than the known sources of support, there were several unknown and hidden supporters, about whom I may never know even during my entire life time. Through this book, I wish to express my sincere heartfelt gratitude and thanks to all such invisible Samaritans. This is the second reason for writing this book.

Following are some of the known people who extended their support whole heartedly. I wish to express my gratitude to all these people. I continue to use the word 'gratitude' because I am not able to find a better word to express my feelings.

1. My family doctor Dr. Vivek Bhosale, who gave me the appropriate initial medical advice;

2. Mr. Navin Gada and Mr. Narendra Gala of Jyoti (India) Metal Industries Pvt. Limited, Palghar;

3. Late Mr. Ananth of Revati Enterprises, Vasai. I will never forget the kind gesture of late Mr. Ananth. I met him only once, as a member of Det Norske Veritas (DNV) audit team, during one of the Quality Management System Audit visits. When Mr. Anant came to know about my treatment, he immediately gave me a high value cheque, even without my asking. I received the cheque on 24/09/2008 and Mr. Anant died due to a massive heart attack on 2/10/2008. I underwent stem cell treatment on 6/10/2008. I was not told about the death of Mr. Ananth for a long time. Just note the miracle here. It appears that Mr. Anant was just waiting to help me, with a last act of charity. I have absolutely no doubt, that his departed soul would be resting in complete peace and tranquility;

4. Late Mr. Gautam Dave of Indian Transformers Company, Boisar, Tarapur. He also died soon after my treatment;

5. Mr. Mukesh Ailani, Executive Engineer, Electrical Engineering Department, Ulhasnagar Municipal Corporation. A dedicated, hard working and non- corrupt, up right government

officer of integrity. He is a perfect role model and a close friend of mine. He mobilized financial support from various sources;

6. Brothers, Mr. Amritesh Vaid and Mr. Parikshit Vaid of Macro Bars and Wires (India) Pvt. Limited, Palghar:

7. Mr. Laxman V Kadam of Vipul Chemicals (India) Private Limited, Mahape;

8. Det Norske Veritas (DNV) auditors- Mr. Avinash Dhavle, Mr. Ramesh Shroff, Mr. Binoy Kurrup, Mr. Rajeev Mandrekar and Mrs. Shiraz:

9. Mr. Panchal and his family. I am greatly indebted to Mr. Ankur, the young son of Mr. Panchal. Mr. Ankur donated platelets on two occasions without any hesitation. Panchals are great human beings and a wonderful family;

10. Members of 'Gayatri Parivar', who enthusiastically came forward to donate platelets. Mr. Panchal was mainly responsible for mobilizing their support;

11. Mr. Deepak Gandhi and his family members at Kalyan. They were our neighbours in Kalyan. We are very close family friends;

12. Mr. P C Yadav and his family members. They were our next door neighbours in Kalyan. The family extended their help and support in several ways; and

13. Dr. G. Vijayaragavan, Ex-Director, Pillai Institute of Management Studies & Research, New Panvel. He extended invaluable moral support during my time of crisis.

I also take this opportunity to express my gratitude and thanks to Dr. Sachin Almel, the doctor who treated and gave me the second life, Dr. Abhey Nene, who was associated during my initial phases of diagnosis, Ms. Avani Bhatia- the social worker attached to the Hinduja Hospital and the entire nursing and support team of the P D Hinduja National Hospital.

The third and the last reason for writing this book is my desire to give back to the society as much as possible so that the cycle of flow is maintained. Innumerable patients are silently enduring immense pain and agony due to lack of finance. The Universe was helpful and kind enough with me. I could raise the required resources through my family members, friends, and charitable persons. A part of the royalty earned through the sale proceeds of this book will be donated to the **'Cancer Fund'** of **National Health & Education Society** (which manages P D Hinduja National Hospital, Mahim, Mumbai, India), a charity organization which is rendering a great service to the cancer patients. This is my humble way of returning something back, though it may be quite insignificant, to the Universe.

In this book, before writing about my experience with the disease I have given a brief introduction about myself. I am fully aware that I am neither a celebrity nor a prominent person to write about myself. I felt it was necessary to give a complete background about me, so that the narration is real, complete and comprehensive. This part of narration is kept as brief as possible.

I have also provided information on other approaches for cancer management. The Information provided in this book are drawn from the published sources of repute. This book should not be substituted for the advice of an expert doctor or a medical consultant.

Each and every word in this book is written by me. I am neither a professional writer nor undergone any sort of formal training in professional writing. I have also not utilized the services of an accomplished writer to write on my behalf. I sincerely believe that though a ghost writer would have made this book a best seller but that definitely would have compromised on the originality and emotional intensity of narration.

I pray for good health to every reader of this book and fast recovery to the patients undergoing the treatment. I would like to conclude this prologue with a meaningful quote:

Trust yourself.
Create the kind of self that you will be happy to live with all your
life.
Make the most of yourself by fanning the tiny, inner spark
of possibility into flames of achievement.

- Golda Meir

C K Sreedharan

'You are what your deep driving desire is.

As is your desire, so is your will,

As is your will, so is your act,

As is your act, so is your DESTINY.'

- Quote from Upanishad

About Multiple Myeloma

'God, grant me the serenity to accept the things I cannot change, the courage to change the things I can, and the wisdom to know the difference.'

-Zen Philosophy.

Cancer is a family or group of diseases that occur in all the human and animal populations and that may arise in any tissue of the body that is composed of potentially dividing cells. The cells in which cancer occurs exhibit two distinct characteristics. One, they no longer exhibit normal growth but instead grow uncontrollably. The second is that they no longer carry out the specific body tasks for which the cells normally exist but instead simply function as cancer cells. The dividing and multiplying, cancer cells transmit these characteristics to their cellular offsprings. As cancer grows, the host animal suffers adverse effects caused by the invasive growth in original tumour site or by metastatic spread to other sites in the body.

Multiple myeloma is a plasma cell (type of blood cell) cancer that usually affects bone marrow.

Bone marrow, stem cells and blood cell formation

Bone marrow

Bone marrow is the soft spongy tissue that lies within the hollow interior of long bones. In adults, marrow in large bones produces new blood cells. Bone marrow forms around 4% of total body weight (around 2.6 kg in a healthy adult).

Human blood cells are produced in the bone marrow. The process through which blood cells are produced is called as 'haemopoiesis.' In case of infants, haemopoiesis process takes place at the centre of all the bones. In adults, it is limited to the hips, ribs, spine, skull and breastbone. For carrying out bone marrow biopsy, the bone marrow is taken from the bone at the back of the hip or the breast bone.

1

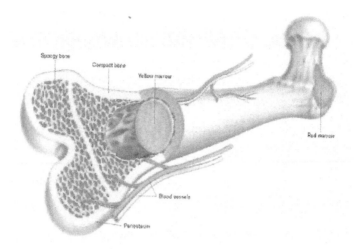

Bone marrow can be considered as the blood cell factory. The main workers at the factory are the blood stem cells. They are relatively small in number but are capable, when stimulated, not only to divide to replicate themselves, but also to grow and divide into slightly more mature stem cells called 'myeloid' stem cells and 'lymphoid' stem cells.

These cells multiply and mature further to produce all the circulating blood cells. There are three main types of blood cells- red cells, white cells and platelets.

Myeloid stem cells develop into red cells, white cells and platelets. Lymphoid stem cells develop into two other types of white cells called T-lymphocytes and B- lymphocytes.

Some B-lymphocytes develop further into plasma cells, which are antibody-producing cells. The antibodies target the bacteria, viruses and other harmful substances entering into the body and help remove them from the body.

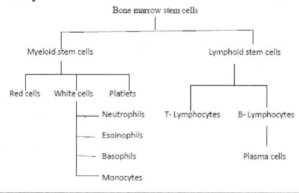

Growth factors and cytokines

All normal blood cells have a limited survival in circulation and need to be replaced on a continuous basis. This means that the bone marrow remains a very active tissue throughout the life of a person. The natural chemicals in the blood called 'growth factors or 'cytokines' control the process of blood cell formation. Different growth factors stimulate the blood stem cells in the bone marrow to produce different types of blood cells.

Blood

Blood consists of blood cells and plasma (plasma- 60% and blood cells-40%).

Plasma is straw coloured fluid part of the blood cells that travel around the body.

Red cells and haemoglobin

Red cells contain haemoglobin which gives blood its red colour and transports oxygen from lungs to all parts of the body.

Haemoglobin also carries carbon dioxide to the lungs where it is breathed out.

White cells

White cells fight infection. There are different types of white cells that fight infection together and in different ways. When white cell count drops below normal the person is at the risk of infection.

Types of white cells:

- Neutrohils- Kill bacteria and fungi.

- Eosinophils- Kill parasites

- Basophils- Work with neutrophils to fight infection

- Monocytes- Work with neutrophils and lymphocytes to fight infection; they also help with antibody production and act as scavengers to remove dead tissue.

-    T-lymphocytes kill viruses, parasites and cancer cells; produce cytokins.

-    B- lymphocytes make antibodies which target microorganisms

Platelets

Platelets are disc-shaped cellular fragments that circulate in blood and play an important function in clot formation. They help to prevent bleeding. If a blood vessel is damaged, say due to a cut, the platelets gather at the site of injury, stick together and form a protective plug to help stop the bleeding. If platelet count drops below certain limit, then the person is at the risk of bleeding and tends to bruise easily. Platelet transfusions may be required to bring the platelet count back to a safe level.

Myeloma or multiple myeloma

It is a type of cancer of plasma cells that usually arises in the bone marrow. Myeloma develops when plasma cells multiply without any proper order, forming collections known as tumours that accumulate in different parts of the body, especially in the bone marrow and on the surfaces of different bones in the body. These tumours secrete chemicals that stimulate other bone marrow cells to remove calcium from the bone. As a result bones can become weaker, more brittle and break more easily.

Under normal conditions, the plasma cells produce 'immunoglobulins' or antibodies that help protect the body from infection and disease. The myeloma cells produce an abnormal type of immunoglobulin called 'paraprotein' or 'M protein.' This can be detected in the blood. Sometimes excessive amount of fragments of immunoglobulins, known as 'light chains,' are produced. These light chains can be detected in the blood and they also appear in the urine. As myeloma cells multiply, they crowd the bone marrow and prevent it from making normal numbers of red cells, white cells and platelets. The myeloma cells can also interfere with the production of normal antibodies. This can make people with myeloma anaemic, more susceptible to infections, to bleeding and bruising more easily.

Plasma cells and immunoglobulins

Plasma cells are a type of blood cell that develops from mature B-lymphocytes in the bone marrow. They play an important role in protecting the body against infection and disease by producing proteins called as 'immunoglobulins,' also known as antibodies. The immunoglobulins are produced by the plasma cells in response to bacteria, viruses and other harmful substances found in the body. Once released into the blood stream, the immunoglobulin circulates about and attaches itself to the target for which it was originally made. This makes it easier for other white blood cells to destroy harmful organisms and other unwanted substances and remove them from the body.

There are different types of plasma cells that develop in response to different types of immunoglobulins specific to the substance recognized as foreign and potentially harmful to the body.

Majority of people diagnosed with myeloma (93%) are above the age of 50. Myeloma is rare under the age of 40 and it has been reported in children and adolescents. Myeloma is more common in men than in women. It is relatively a rare disease. It accounts for approximately 1% of all cancers and 10% of all blood and bone marrow cancers.

There is no known reason for the cause of the disease. It is not contagious. In most cases people who are diagnosed with myeloma have no family history of the disease. There are certain factors that may put some people at a higher risk of developing this disease. These include exposure to high doses of radiation and ongoing exposure to certain industrial or environmental chemicals.

Symptoms

Symptoms of multiple myeloma depend on how advanced the disease is. In the initial stages, there may be no symptoms at all and the disease may be accidentally picked up during a routine blood test.

Symptoms related to myeloma are described with the mnemonic-CRAB. It means:

- High blood **C**alcium

- Poor **R**enal or kidney function

- **A**naemia

- **B**one pain or bone lesions: The most common symptom of myeloma is bone pain. This is usually felt in the back or ribs and may be made worse by movement. Bone pain is usually the result of the gradual erosion of bone caused by the substances secreted by the myeloma cells. Over a period of time bones can become weakened and thinned and holes may develop, increasing the risk of fracture of the bone.

When bone tissue is damaged, calcium is released from the bone into the blood stream. An excess of calcium in the blood is called 'hypercalcaemia.' If a person has higher than normal calcium level in the blood, he / she may feel nauseated, constipated, thirsty or even confused. The increased calcium level is referred as serum calcium level > 0.25 mmol / L above the upper limit of normal or a level that is > 2.75 mmol / L.

Bone lesions include:
- Lytic lesions (areas of bone damage);
- Osteoporosis (thinning of bones); and
- Compression fracture of bones.

Other symptoms of myeloma manifest when these cancer cells crowd the bone marrow and prevent it from making normal red cells, white cells and platelets. This can lead to anaemia, frequent or repeated infections, bleeding or bruising more easily.

The patients with CRAB symptoms require active treatment. The patients may also be treated, if any of the following conditions are observed:

1. Bone marrow plasma observed to be > 60%.
2. Kappa-to-lambda ratio is > 100, based on serum testing, with absolute values > 100 mg /L or 10 mg / dL.
3. Bone lesions seen on MRI, or PET –CT imaging.

Diagnosis of myeloma

Diagnosis is based on the information and other details gathered from a number of different tests like blood tests, urine tests, bone marrow biopsy, X-ray, MRI and other more specialized bone imaging tests.

Blood and urine tests

'Serum protein' and 'serum electrophoresis' tests are carried out to measure the amount and type of paraprotein in the person's blood. The blood sample is usually taken out from the vein in the arm or in the hand.

'Urine electrophoresis' is a test used to measure the amount of protein in the urine. The patient under investigation is asked to collect the total urine passed in a 22- hour period so that the amount of paraprotein, also known as light chains that are passed out during the period can be measured.

The amount of paraprotein present in the blood and / or urine reflects the extent of myeloma at the time of diagnosis. This information is used as a baseline which is used to compare with other results to check the progress of the patient.

Bone marrow biopsy

This involves taking out a sample of the bone marrow, usually from the back of the hip bone to count the number of plasma cells present and to see how well the bone marrow is functioning. Under normal conditions plasma cells make up less than 5% of all the cells within the bone marrow. In myeloma patient, the number is usually over 30% or more.

Creatinine test

Creatinine is a chemical normally excreted in urine. Blood level of creatinine is measured to assess how well the kidneys are functioning.

High levels of blood calcium usually indicate that bone tissue is being damaged.

Complete blood count (CBC)

It is a simple blood test that measures the number of red cells, white cells and platelets in circulation and examines their size and shape. This helps to assess how well the bone marrow is functioning and whether or not normal blood cells are being affected by the myeloma.

Measurement of beta-2 microglobulin

Measuring the blood level of beta-2 microglobulin, a special protein found in myeloma, provides a useful indicator of the likely course of the disease.

High levels of beta-2 microglobulin indicate the presence of a large amount of myeloma cells, and / or the kidney damage.

Measurement of other proteins

Levels of other proteins like lactate dehydrogenase (LDH) and C- reactive protein are also measured to assess the amount of myeloma in the body and how fast it is growing.

Stage of the disease

Stage of myeloma refers to the extent of disease in the body. Knowing the stage is important to decide the best method of treatment.

There are three possible stages of myeloma. Stage I refers to the early stage. Stage III refers to more advanced disease where there is a large amount of myeloma in the body.

International Myeloma Working Group (IMWG) has developed a simple staging system for myeloma based on the level of beta-2 microglobulin and albumin in the blood.

IMWG staging system for myeloma

Stage I

Low levels of beta-2 microglobulin (< 3.5 mg / L)

Normal blood albumin level (≥ 35 g / L).

Stage II
Moderate level of beta-2 microglobulin (3.5 mg / L to 5.5 mg /L)
Reduced blood albumin level (≤ 35 g / L)

Stage III

High level of beta-2 microglobulin (> 5.5 mg / L)

Types of myeloma

Myeloma can be classified according to how the disease is distributed in the body. In majority of the cases myeloma is found in multiple bone marrow sites at diagnosis, which is why the disease is often called 'multiple myeloma.'

Sometimes an isolated collection of myeloma cell is found in only one site. When this happens, the disease is described as a solitary myeloma or solitary plasmacytoma.

Cure

Although there is currently no cure for myeloma, it can be treated successfully. Developments of new and improved treatments mean that the outlook for people with myeloma is gradually improving. The treatment can often slow down the progression of the disease, sometimes for several years.

Common terms used

Complete remission

The treatment has been so successful that paraprotein can no longer be detected in blood or urine using standard tests, and that the percentage of plasma cells in the bone marrow has returned to normal.

Plateau phase (remission plateau)

Progress of myeloma has been halted and paraprotein level is stable. Myeloma is not getting any worse or any better with treatment.

The length of time that the remission (or plateau phase) lasts varies from person to person and myeloma may well reappear, even after a long time. For this reason, regular checkups are necessary while the patient is in remission.

Relapse - The myeloma has reappeared.

Treatment to control myeloma

Chemotherapy

It is the main form of treatment used to control myeloma. The aim here is to progressively reduce the amount of myeloma to as low a level as possible.

There are many ways of giving chemotherapy. Some chemo drugs are given in tablet form .Others are given intravenously, usually in the arm or hand.

High-dose chemotherapy

It is often used for people who are young and generally under 75 years of age and have no other serious illness. This is because high-dose chemo has been shown to be more effective than standard dose chemo in reducing the amount of myeloma in the body and prolonging a remission.

A side effect of high-dose chemotherapy is the destruction of the normal bone marrow, which needs to be replaced with an 'autologous bone marrow transplant' or 'peripheral blood stem transplant.'

An autologous transplant is now the standard treatment for many people diagnosed with myeloma. This type of treatment involves collecting stem cells, from the blood stream of the patient, storing them and giving them back to the patient after the high-dose chemotherapy.

In a small number of cases an 'allogeneic bone marrow or 'peripheral blood stem cell transplant' using a suitably matched donor may be considered.

Side-effects of chemotherapy

Chemotherapy kills cells that multiply quickly, such as cancer cells. It also causes damage to fast-growing normal cells, including hair cells and cells in the mouth, gut and bone marrow. Side-effects and their severity vary from person to person and on the type of chemotherapy used and how an individual responds to it.

Effects on the bone marrow

Chemotherapy also affects bone marrow's ability to produce adequate number of blood cells- white cells, red cells and platelets. As a result, the blood count (the number of white cells, red cells and platelets) in the patient's blood will generally fall after the

treatment. The length of time it takes for the blood count to fall
and recover mainly depends on the type of chemotherapy given.

White cells

White cells count may go down after the chemotherapy treatment.
During this time the patient will be at a higher risk of developing
infection. While the white blood cell count is low, the patient
shall take necessary precautions to prevent infection.

Platelets

Platelet count may become low due to chemotherapy and patient can
bruise and bleed more easily. If the platelet count is low, the doctor may
advice a platelet transfusion to reduce the risk of bleeding until platelet
count recovers.

Red blood cells

Red blood cells counts may drop and the patient may become
anaemic. Doctor may prescribe a blood transfusion.

Radiotherapy

Radiotherapy treatment uses high energy x-rays to kill the cancer
cells and shrink the tumours. It is generally regarded as local therapy
since it only destroys cancer cells in the treated area. It can be used in
a number of ways to treat myeloma. In some cases isolated masses of
myeloma cells like plasmacytoma may be successfully treated using
radiotherapy alone. It is also used to treat areas of bone that have
become weakened due to myeloma. This helps to reduce pain, and the
risk of bone fractures.

Obesity is also believed to affect cancer cell metabolism and immune clearance, all of which can contribute to the growth and spread of tumours. Obesity increases the risk of inflammation, which is associated with cancer.

- Mumbai Mirror dated 4 September, 2017.

Not just medicine: Doctors enlist yoga in India's fight against cancer. Yoga helps manage symptoms as well as pain:

'It is not just physical pain but also psychological, social and spiritual trauma that cancer patients experience. All this needs a holistic approach towards treatment.'

- Dr. Prabha Seshachar, S-VYASA, Bangalore.

'Yoga provides psychological relief. We have seen cases where patients have seen improvement in health when yoga is practiced along with chemotherapy or radiation. The side-effects can be reduced.'

- Dr. Amit Singh, Chief Medical Officer, S-VYASA, Bangalore.

References

1. Information given in this section is adopted from the booklet, 'Understanding Myeloma- A guide for patients and families,' published by Leukaemia Foundation, Australia. http://www.cancer.net/cancer-types/multiple-myeloma/stages

   (Readers are strongly advised to refer information provided in the above website)

2. 'Lower your cancer risk now' by Dr. Mitchell L Gaynor and Jerry Hickey.

About my family

' Become a possibilitarian. No matter how dark things seem to be or actually are, raise your sights and possibilities-always see them, for they're always there.'

-Norman Vincent Peale

Chirichingi Narasimhachar Krishna Iyengar, my father, was born in Melkote, in Mandya district of present Karnataka State, in the year 1923. Melkote is one of the important and holy places for Shree Vaishnava Iyengar community. Shree. Ramanuja, the tenth century sage, hailed as a great revolutionary religious guru, had spent more than ten years in Melkote, spreading Vaishnava philosophy. My father was born in a humble and an extremely orthodox iyengar family.

Like any other Brahmin children in the village, my father went to school as well as to Sanskrit patashala. The Brahmin children (both boys and girls) compulsorily went to Sanskrit patashala in the morning and went to school afterwards. By the time the student completed high school education, the student also acquired fair levels of proficiency in scriptures, Vedas and other Sanskrit literature. My father was one such scholar who had acquired the highest level of proficiency in Sanskrit.

My father was a studious student and one of the very few from the village, who studied beyond higher secondary level. In those days, majority of the Brahmin students, dropped out at various levels of school education. Only a few students progressed beyond school and completed graduate level education. My father was a rank holder in under graduation level and he was offered admission in the prestigious Government Engineering College (presently Vishveshwarayya College of Engineering) Bangalore. He selected civil engineering branch.

During that time India's freedom movement was in full swing. My father and some of his friends were also drawn into the movement. Mahatma Gandhi launched the 'Quit India' movement in 1942. My father also actively plunged into the movement. My father was arrested and imprisoned in Mandya Central Jail.

My father spent about six months in the jail. Kadri Shamanna, a famous personality from Karnataka, was my father's jail mate and subsequently both of them became very close friends. Due to the intervention of some Indian and British intellectuals all the imprisoned student agitators were released and were permitted to continue their studies. Perhaps, the experience of hardship in jail life made my father a simple, humble human being and a person of highest integrity and honesty. These imbibed values helped my father to remain ethical and a person of integrity in his government job, even though the job provided plenty of opportunities to indulge in corrupt practices.

After successfully completing Bachelor of Engineering in civil engineering, my father got a job in Public Works Department (PWD), a state government job, in the present State of Tamilnadu.

It is appropriate to introduce my maternal grandfather at this juncture. My grandfather's name was P.S. Soundararajan. Unlike my father, who fought against the British rule, my grandfather worked with British people during his employment in Indian Railways. Even though he had limited school education, he acquired excellent command over English language and spoke the language like a native British.

My grandfather was blessed with seven daughters. My father first married the eldest daughter of my grandfather, who was my mother's eldest sister. In my Tamil language she is called as 'Periamma' meaning elder mother. My periamma was a trained classical bharatanatyam dancer and we were told that she was an excellent, graceful and an elegant dancer. Unfortunately, my periamma was destined to die young and she died after two years of married life.

My grandfather liked my father very much and he consented to the remarriage of my father with his third daughter that was my mother. My father married my mother in 1952.

My mother was short, just under four feet and ten inches, but was very dynamic and bold. She faced many tough and challenging situations in her life, but handled each difficult situation with patience and dignity.

My elder brother, Ravindran was born in 1952. He pursued PhD in Geology and retired from service in 2013 as General Manager-ONGC, New Panvel. He is now settled in Chennai.

My elder sister Radha was born in 1954. She pursued Masters in Chemistry and worked as professor in many colleges in Chennai. She is now settled in Chennai.

I was born in 1958 and I am going to write about myself in the subsequent chapter.

My younger sister Mythily was born in 1962. She completed PhD in Chemistry and presently working as Head of the Department in Maharani's College, Bangalore.

My father died on 9-09-2011, after a brief period of illness. He led a disease free life for almost 89 years. His death was reported in main Kannada news papers, with the caption, 'A veteran freedom fighter passes away.'

My mother had a setback in 1996. One of her kidney's had to be removed due to cancer. She lived with one kidney for the rest of her life. She passed away on 28.08.2016 due to cancer.

I am really blessed and thank God for giving me such wonderful parents, grandparents, loving, caring and supporting brother, sisters and their husbands. Along with them my own family members- my beautiful wife, two lovely daughters, my brother-in-law and my elder son-in law who is like a son to me, form my strong support pillars. They all solidly stood by me, and looked after me with great love and affection during my period of crisis and distress.

The family support system is another important factor which helped me to recover fast and become a normal person again without much difficulty.

I have struggled in my life and success is still eluding me even after acquiring a degree in mechanical engineering from one of the reputed engineering colleges of the country and acquiring many more qualifications and wide and extensive industrial experience. Sometimes I have an intense feeling that life is cruel and unfair and it supports only the undeserving. But a great realization dawned on me when I happened to see the following quote:

> Happiness and success, do they go together?
> Happiness is not always through success.
> Equally, the constant pursuit of success is sure unhappiness,
> But we have to find the balance
>
> - Amy Chua

Mind over body:

It is proven beyond doubt that there is a constant communication between the mind and body. Every thought that crosses our mind or every word that we utter, signals the body accordingly and the body responds by manifesting those thoughts. This is exactly why positive affirmations / mantras work like magic. By constantly focusing on the positive aspects of life or expressing gratitude towards little things, we automatically train our brain to think positive. Even when it comes to health, one cannot take the 'mind' out of the equation of prevention and healing.

Most diseases these days may be connected to a malfunction in the body's spirit and mind. It is all 'psychosomatic' meaning it stems from the mind, and then by constantly thinking about, we create a perfect environment for the disease to actually breed. So if you picture a disease for yourself- you are likely to invite it. Instead, picture yourself as a healthy and happy person and you are likely to be so.

- Luke Coutinho, MD, Alternative medicine (Times of India, 31 December, 2017)

My early years

'One must not forget that recovery is brought about not by the physician, but by the sick man himself. He heals himself, by his own power, exactly as he walks by means of his own power, or eats, or thinks, breaths or sleeps.'
-George Groddeck, The Book of the It, 1923.

I was born as a third child to my parents after my elder brother and elder sister. I was born in Trivellore, Chenglepet district of Tamilnadu state. I was a normal and a healthy boy.

I grew up with my parents till I was seven years old. My parents used to visit Melkote, my father's native place every year. This visit used to happen generally during the summer vocation and my parents used to take the entire family along with them. During one such visits, due to the insistence of my grandmother, my parents decided to leave me at Melkote, so that, at least one person in the family learned Sanskrit by attending Sanskrit patashala.

I completed my school education up to seventh standard in Melkote. I studied in the village school and simultaneously studied Sanskrit for about four years, thereby acquiring a little proficiency in Sanskrit.

I visited my parents once in a year during summer vocation. Only during such short visits I stayed with my parents, brother and sisters. I was really deprived off the childhood happiness and pleasure of growing with close family members. Looking back now, I am really sad that I missed out the best part of my childhood.

My father's job was transferrable to different parts of Tamilnadu state, and he was transferred to a new place every three to four years. Due to these frequent transfers,
my brother and sisters were left with our maternal grandparents to ensure uninterrupted school education. My grandparents lived in Trivellore, a small town about 45 km from the city of Chennai.

After completing seventh standard at Melkote, during the summer vocation, I came to visit my parents. My father was posted at

Cuddalore. By this time, I had developed a strong desire to stay with my parents, brother and sisters. I refused to go back to Melkote and my parents also supported me. It was decided to admit me in the same school at Trivellore, where my brother and elder sister studied. I shifted my schooling from Melkote –Karnataka State to Trivellore, a school in Tamilnadu. This gave me an opportunity to learn two south Indian languages- Kannada and Tamil. Like my brother and sisters, I also started living with my grandparents at Trivellore.

My entire family-my parents, my brother and sisters and I are greatly indebted to our maternal grandparents- Soundararajan our grandfather and Kuppammal our grandmother. For us our grandparents are more adorable than our parents. They played an important and critical role in our upbringing and created a powerful protective shield around us.

I completed my eighth and ninth standard schooling at Trivellore. While my younger sister and I stayed with our grandparents my elder brother and elder sister pursued their college education at Chennai, staying with our aunt- my mother's younger sister.

My grandfather decided to shift closer to Chennai city, so that his grandchildren could pursue their college education without much difficulty. We shifted to Perambur, a suburb of Chennai City in the year 1972. After completing my first term of tenth standard in Trivellore, I joined a school in Perambur during second term of tenth standard. I completed my tenth standard in Perambur.

At that time, my father was posted in Virudhunagar; a town situated about 60 km from Madurai City. My father wanted me to pursue my school final, which was eleventh standard in those days, at Virudhunagar so that he could coach me personally. I shifted to Virudhunagar and joined K V Shala High School. I stood first in Virudhunagar district and the school honoured me with a gold medal.

I had to come back to Chennai to pursue my Pre-University level, as my father was transferred. My grandfather was very keen that I joined Vivekananda College at Mylapore, managed by Ramakrishna Mutt. Since I secured a very high percentage in my eleventh standard I got the admission very easily in Vivekananda College.

I passed Pre University Course in the year 1975 with excellent percentage. I wanted to pursue engineering after my pre university. At that time, there were only a few engineering colleges in the state apart from one IIT. That was the time when students from forward communities faced acute problems in getting admission to the professional courses due to high levels of reservation provided for other communities. I appeared for the IIT entrance examination but could not qualify. I was dejected and lost all hopes of getting admission into engineering.

My grandfather came in contact with a person, whose son was studying engineering at BITS Pilani, Rajasthan. I applied and got admission into the five year integrated programme. This was in the year 1975.

BITS Pilani followed a different pattern of five years integrated programme at that time. That pattern was totally different from what it is today. The first two years were common to all streams of study. The actual branching into various streams like engineering, management, commerce, science etc used to take place only after the end of second year. Allocation into various streams was done based on relative performance of the students, demand for a particular stream and the availability of seats. There was considerable uncertainty and risk involved in getting the desired stream. With that system, a student, who joined the institute with the intention of pursuing a degree in engineering, could end up pursuing totally a different stream of study, say a management or a science stream, against one's wish.

My cumulative grade point average (CGPA) dropped to 5.5 by the end of second year, and I was uncertain about getting engineering stream. I told my parents that I might not get engineering stream and would like to discontinue at BITS. I once again applied to PSG College of Engineering, Coimbatore and Delhi College of Engineering, Delhi.

I got admission into BE-Agriculture in PSG College of Engineering and also admission into BSc (Engg.)- Mechanical in Delhi College of Engineering. I decided to take up engineering in Delhi College of Engineering, Delhi.

I shifted from BITS Pilani to Delhi College of Engineering, to pursue mechanical engineering stream. I had to commence right from the first year again due to the autonomous nature of BITS and my two years of study was not recognized by the Delhi University.

The decision to discontinue at BITS was the first major blunder I committed in my life. After I discontinued and joined at Delhi College of Engineering, the students from my batch revolted and agitated against BITS for the way it conducted its five year integrated programme as many of the students with the intention of pursuing engineering degree did not get engineering. There was a big showdown, and BITS was finally forced to change the pattern of its integrated programme. All engineering aspirants were offered engineering stream and all my friends who faced uncertainty could get into engineering stream. I still regret a lot for the hasty decision I took at that time. In the process, I not only lost two precious years but also the opportunity to complete engineering in a world class institute.

(With the BITS friends, I stand second from left, in the first row)

I still cherish my two years stint (1975-1977) at BITS. BITS completely changed my studying habits. I started focusing more on learning concepts rather than memorizing. My proficiency in English language improved to a great extent. I enrolled in National Cadet Corps (NCC), and got trained in riffle shooting. I could emerge as a fairly sharp riffle shooter. Memories of 'Oasis' the annual cultural festival, the weekly screening of films in the auditorium, the Saraswati temple, museum, Shivganga- the artificial waterway, Connaught place- the mini shopping center, Jayashree- the small theatre in the Pilani village, the free roaming, dancing peacocks and peahens- which were abundant in the campus, still pleasantly haunt me.

I also had an extensive friends circle. I still remember the days I spent with my wonderful friends- Siddharthan, Nagaraj, Manoharan, Bhaskar, Raghunath, Krishna Murthy, Venkatraman, Vinod Kumar and many others. I still maintain contact with some of the above friends. Even today, I proudly cherish and boast about my two years stint at BITS, Pilani.

Like BITS, Pilani Delhi College of Engineering (DCE) is also a reputed engineering college. Though I lost two academic years, I had one consolation- I got admission in mechanical engineering stream, which was my dream and ambition. During my time the college was in Kashmeri Gate, close to Inter State Bus Terminus (ISBT). Later, the college was shifted to Delhi University area. The duration of engineering programme was five years, comprising of ten semesters. During the first three semesters I stayed with my uncle (father's younger brother), who was at Delhi at that time. In the beginning of fourth semester, I shifted to college hostel, as my uncle was transferred to Bangalore.

DCE had several experienced and competent teaching faculty. I was fortunate enough to be taught by the eminent professors like Prof. P L Balaney- an authority on thermodynamics and steam engines, Dr. Sachdeva, Prof. Mandal, Dr. Venkateshwaralu and Prof. Saluja. They were all professors of high calibre and I still remember the excellent lecture sessions conducted by them.

Hostel life was fantastic and enjoyable. I still maintain contact with many of my adorable friends. I would like to mention a few of their names- CR Narayanan (appe), Sundararajan Chotu), Balram (Ballu), Srinivas, Jerry Kapoor, Balan, Shivarama Krishnan (ANS), CV Raman, Aseem Malhotra, Ganesh, Shivasubramanian, Umesh Rai, Srivatsan, TV Subramanian, R Sridhar, Balasubramanian (Balls), V Sreedharan (Lee)- my dear roommate. Each one had a pet name and I was called 'mama' as I was senior to everyone by about two years due to my stint at BITS.

I am really very happy to mention here that both my BITS Pilani and DCE friends are exceptionally successful in their professional life and are occupying top most positions in their organizations. God bless them all!

Like my BITS Pilani memories I relish several wonderful memories of DCE, Delhi. I actively participated in all the college elections supporting my friends, was a regular member of the organizing committee of 'Engifest'- the annual college cultural festival and was an energetic group leader of National Service Scheme (NSS). I was also a member of hiking club and went on trekking to several wonderful locations.

Some of the trekking locations were- Ninetal, Kullu-Manali-Rohtang Pass and Sariska wild life sanctuary. I was fit and healthy and had good stamina to undertake the above trekking adventures.

Within you are all the elements of a fully functioning department of defense. Like citizen-soldiers, the cells of your immune system quickly march in their millions and tens of millions to any site of infection and slaughter the invaders.

They have guards posted to spot the first sign of trouble, they have a communication network, they have commanders who decide who they'll attack and who is in possession of the password and therefore free to come or go.

They have bases where the troops stay when they're not fighting, they have the ability to explosively multiply their numbers-the equivalent of a draft instituted during the direct emergency- and they declare peace and partly demobilize after the war is won. They have determination, self-sacrifice, and the will to win.

Malignant cells are one of the things this highly aggressive standing army has the ability and the desire to destroy.

- Dr. Mitchell L Gaynor in his book, 'Lower your cancer risk now!'

Purify indoor air naturally

A number of air pollutants exist indoors like nitrogen oxides, sulphur dioxide, carbon monoxide, volatile and semi-volatile organic compounds and microorganism. These air pollutants can cause health problems ranging from simple allergies, asthama to cancers. Here is a natural way to purify the air in homes:

Indoor plants: Keeping house plants is the best method of air purification in less or non-ventilated buildings. Areca palm removes carbon dioxide and converts into oxygen. It is good to keep four shoulder-high plants per person and it is necessary to wipe the leaves at least once in a week. Mother-in-law's tongue is called the bedroom plant, because it converts carbon dioxide into oxygen at night and can purify chemical-laden indoor air.

- Mumbai Mirror, Mumbai edition dated 28 November, 2017

Cervical cancer

Cervical cancer is the second most common cancer among women in India, after breast cancer. Nearly 67,000 women die of cervical cancer in India. It is detected in advanced stages in 70% of patients in India. 25% of patients in world are in India.

Cervix is the lower part of the uterus and connects it to the birth canal. Human papillomavius (HPV) is the most important risk factor. HPV is mainly transmitted through sexual contact. Infections usually clear up without any medical intervention within a few months, but a small proportion of infections with certain HPV types can persist and progress to cancer.

If a cervical tumour is more than 4 cm, chemotherapy should be the first choice of treatment and no resource should be wasted in surgically removing it, say Tata Memorial doctors.

- Times of India, Mumbai edition dated 8 February, 22018.

(On the way to Rohtang Pass)

(L to R- CR Narayanan, me, V Sridharan)

Purify indoor air naturally

Essential oils are one of the easiest remedies for indoor pollution. It can reduce the virulence of the indoor pollutants to a great extent. Recent studies suggest that two drops of any of these oils- thyme, bay, cinnamon, clove, mint and oregano – can be mixed with one litre of water and can be sprayed inside the living area. Another method is keeping the essential oil in a small vessel and allowing it to evaporate inside the room.

At Rohtang Pass

Beas river (L to R- me, CR Narayanan, V Sridharan)

Tent near Beas Kund
(L to R- CR Narayanan, V Sridharan, me)

I completed my graduation in mechanical engineering in April 1982. Friends separated as each one of us went in search of job. For a couple of years we remained in contact, subsequently only a few continued to remain in contact, and many vanished without any trace.

My professional life

'I am a little deaf, a little blind, a little impotent, and top of this are two or three abominable infirmities, but nothing destroys my hope.'

-Voltaire

My first job was at Metal Lamp Caps (India) Pvt. Limited, Bangalore. The company was a leading manufacturer of electrical lamp accessories. I joined as a graduate trainee engineer. I moved to Bangalore in August 1982.

My father retired from his job in 1978. After his retirement, my father shifted to Bangalore as he got a job as a consultant in a consultancy company called Torr Steel India Limited. Later in 1980, he was approached by a leading construction company CT Ramanathan & Company, to join as Chief Engineer. The company bagged a huge project construction work at Mysore, State of Karnataka. The project was for a company called Machinery Manufacturers Corporation (MMC), in which Mr. Keshub Mahindra of Mahindra & Mahindra Company had a substantial holding. MMC was to manufacture a range of textile machines like- draw frame, speed frame, ring frame and textile machinery accessories.

My father accepted the job offered by CT Ramanathan & Company and shifted to Mysore. He stayed at Yelwal, a village close to the project site.

My father felt that MMC could give me a better career prospects. I also stayed away from my parents for several years and wanted to be with my parents. I applied for a job at MMC and was offered a job as a graduate trainee engineer, an entry level position in the organization.

I joined MMC on 08.12.1982. Initially MMC seemed to be a good organization to work with and showed good potential to scale new heights. The firm entered into a technical collaboration with Marzoli an Italian firm, a world leader in the manufacture of the entire range of textile machineries.

Unfortunately from the year 1985 onwards, the prospects of textile industries in the country started showing a downward trend, and a recessionary trend started deepening. The incompetent, unprofessional and corrupt top management personnel further destroyed the prospects and competitiveness of MMC. MMC struggled to maintain its operations profitable. The company revamped the top management and brought in a new management. But this action came too late since the company was already in a hopeless situation.

Meanwhile my marriage was finalized with Shanthi, who hailed from Srirangam. Shanthi had just completed her B.Com in Seethalaxmi Ramaswamy College, Trichy. The marriage took place on 07.06.1987 in Srirangam. I have no hesitation in writing that I am the luckiest and a blessed person in the entire universe to get such a wonderful woman as my life partner.

Sometime in September 1986, Bureau of Indian Standards (BIS), a Central Government organization called for applications for various positions in the organization. I applied for the post of Assistant Director, an entry level position in the organization. I was called for an interview on 05.06.1987, which was very close to my date of marriage. But a riot broke out in Delhi and the interview was indefinitely postponed.

Surprisingly in March 1988, I received the interview call again from BIS and was asked to appear for an interview at BIS headquarters at New Delhi. I appeared for the interview and was selected. I received the appointment letter from BIS, in April 1988, advising me to report for duty on or before 14.07.1988. My place of posting was Mumbai. I decided to resign from MMC and join BIS.

But there was no need for me to resign from MMC. The new management decided to close down the operations of the firm, as it was no longer viable and profitable. Finally MMC once and for all suspended its operations with effect from 08.05.1988.

I came to Bombay and joined BIS at Andheri- East. My college mate and a close friend, Sundararajan (Chotu) was at Cheddha Nagar, Chembur. He was kind enough to accommodate me in his flat temporarily. This was a great help for a newcomer like me to Bombay city as it gave me sufficient time to look for an accommodation.

My first daughter, Saranya was born on 02.08.1988 in Srirangam. I managed to get a flat on rent in Dombivli, a suburb of Mumbai. I brought my wife and daughter to Mumbai in January 1989 and shifted to Dombivli. BIS office was in Andheri-East and I commuted to work in suburban local train network- the Mumbai's lifeline.

An unfortunate incidence took place in my wife's family- Shanthi's elder brother- Rajan-my elder brother-in-law died in a road accident in Srirangam in September 1989. My second brother-in-law, Murali got a job in Mumbai. My father-in-law was retired and mother-in-law was totally shattered after the death of Rajan. My in-law's family decided to leave Srirangam and shift to Mumbai along with my second brother-in-law, Murali. The family also rented a flat in Dombivli, in the same building where I was staying.

BIS is a national standards formulation and ISI mark product certification body. The main objectives of the organization are to ensure that the consumers get reliable, safe and quality products. I worked in the product certification department. The companies which use ISI mark on their products are under the surveillance of BIS. ISI mark on some products / components / accessories dealing with liquefied petroleum gas (LPG) - gas cylinders, valves, and regulators are mandatory. Similarly other products like electrical switches, electrical motors, pumps, high pressure cylinders are also under compulsory certification. BIS closely monitors process control measures adopted by the companies under mandatory certification. The control measures may involve raw material release, stage inspection and final batch inspection.

In April 1992, I was allotted an official quarters at Shristi Complex, Mira Road. I accepted the allotment and shifted to Mira Road. In June 1993, I was promoted as Deputy Director.

BIS gave me an excellent opportunity for visiting several reputed industries like Everest Kanto Cylinders, Ceat Tyres, Bombay Tyres, Voltas, Crompton & Greaves, VIP Industries, Vidhyut Metallics, Bharat Bijlee, Bombay Wire Ropes, Rocket Engineering, Anchor, Mohata & Heckel, Mukand Steel, Kosan Engineering, Vanaz Engineering, IBP and many more. I visited a wide spectrum of industries, practically covering every industry sector. I interacted with several leading industrialists, industry experts and consultants. I learnt about various business models, importance of specification in building quality in a product, sampling plans, different types of nondestructive testing and process control methods. I also learnt how to prepare specification for a product and scheme of testing and inspection for manufacture of a product. I attended several conferences, workshops and extensive training sessions. This type of extensive exposure helped me to a great extent subsequently when I started my own consultancy services. BIS experience gave me market credibility, industry acceptance, strong professional image and respectability.

The initial enthusiasm slowly started waning as I continued to work in BIS. I felt that I was in a wrong place even though the job was respectable, secured, gave a fantastic designation handsome salary, provided relaxed work environment and finally lot of opportunities for making money through corrupt practices. I was uncomfortable and unhappy with the well spread out systematic corrupt practices throughout the organization.

Earlier BIS was called as 'Indian Standards Institution.' It was an autonomous organization, mainly responsible for the preparation of national standards. Subsequently Government of India enacted BIS Act 1986. The name was changed to Bureau of Indian Standards and was brought under the Ministry of Civil and Food Supplies, thereby making it a central government establishment. The changed status brought along with it the so called government culture, indifference, lack of accountability and the worst evil of them all – a well networked, systematic, organization wide corruption and malpractices.

I would like to mention here that there were a few upright and honest officers who did not accept any favours, but their number was ridiculously small.

While in BIS, I frequently used to visit a company called Expo Gas Containers Limited, a public limited company in Murbad, about 90 km from Mumbai city. The company was a leading manufacturer of LPG cylinders and fabricator of pressure vessels, LPG bullets, spheres, columns, mounded LPG tanks and heat exchangers. The company had some quality issues in its LPG cylinder division and its production was suspended by the public sector oil companies-Hindustan Petroleum Corporation Limited (HPCL) and Bharat Petroleum Corporation Limited (BPCL). The company was looking for a senior person, who could guide the company out of the problem of suspension and also would improve the company's image in the market.

The corrupt system and the repetitive nature of the job at BIS unsettled me. Two of my colleagues and close friends- Talukdar and Amit Palit, quit BIS and joined private companies at better positions with higher salary packages. These resignations further strengthened my resolve to quit BIS.

Mr. SS Mewawala, the Managing Director of Expo Gas Containers Limited came to know about my intention to leave BIS. I had met him on several occasions during my inspection visits to the firm. He knew about my expertise, competence, integrity and honesty. One day Mewawala came to BIS office and expressed his desire to appoint me as the General Manager (Works), the third top position in the organization after the Managing Director and Executive Director.

I completely knew about the company and also the top management. I also felt that the company could give me a good career growth. I quoted a salary; almost three times more than what I was getting at BIS. This was before the implementation of the fifth pay commission's recommendations and salaries were considerably low in government organizations. To my surprise Mewawala accepted my terms and conditions and asked me to join the company immediately.

I did not consult any of my family members. My BIS colleagues and friends strongly advised me to rethink about my decision.

My wife was too young at that time and she was not very clear about the repercussions. I decided to quit BIS and join Expo Gas Containers Limited. I resigned from BIS and joined Expo Gas Containers on 1.07.1995. This was the second biggest blunder I committed in my life. My father never forgave me for my reckless decision and taunted me as long as he was alive.

But I was elated and felt at the top of the world as I had become the General Manager of a public limited company, a senior position in the organization, at a very young age of 37 years. I felt that it was just the beginning of a great career ahead.

At Expo Gas Containers, I worked with missionary zeal and enthusiasm. During my tenure (1995-1999) the company made quick progress and touched many milestones. I was instrumental in getting the fabrication shop approved from several reputed agencies like Engineers India Limited, Jacobs H&G, Projects & Development

India Limited, Toyo Engineering, Godrej, Navin Flourine and IBR. There was not even a single quality complaint in any of the cylinders manufactured. As an Ex-BIS expert I brought respectability to the company and enhanced the reputation of the company. I brought in professional management. The Managing Director and the Executive Director hailed me as a great manager and attributed the success of the company to my efforts and skilful management. For the first time in the history of Expo Gas Containers Limited, the company touched a turnover of Rs. 26 crore in the year 1996-1997. I also implemented Quality Management System as per ISO: 9001-1995 International Standard in the organization, without the help of an external consultant, which was a great feat. The management appreciated me and rewarded me with a substantial increment.

As I mentioned in the beginning, I was not destined to be successful in any of my chosen field. A new person by name Nimkar joined the organization as a project manager in the year 1998. He was scheming and treacherous. He was over ambitious and joined the company with the intention of heading the factory by displacing me. As a project manager he visited the factory regularly. He started feeding the management with wrong and twisted information regarding the way the factory was managed. Initially, the management did not take his dubious reporting seriously. Nimkar systematically started polarizing my subordinates against me. The management also subverted funds with malicious intentions and did not provide the basic requirements to the factory in time. The company defaulted in some of the projects of Mitsubishi and projects under Engineers India Limited. Factory became the scapegoat for all the wrong doings of the management.

The Managing Director and the Executive Director (who was just a puppet and incompetent), started harassing me. Mr. I K Paharia, who was Director- Marketing, solidly supported me .He was a seasoned and an experienced professional. Mr. Paharia was also a straight forward and a no-nonsense person just like me. Nimkar created such a situation in the factory that I did not want to continue in the company. I submitted my resignation in June 1999.

When I joined the company, the firm had just come out with its maiden public issue and the company's issue was oversubscribed. The company became a public limited company. Before the public issue, Mewawala struggled as an industrialist and was unsuccessful as an entrepreneur. In the initial stages he incurred extensive losses due to his ambitious plan to produce and market pressure cookers. The entire project flopped badly. Mewawala slowly diversified into fabrication of pressure vessel which gradually changed his fortune. To his credit, Mewawala was from a wealthy Muslim business community and an electronics engineer from Bombay IIT. He was a humble, devout Muslim and did namaz as per the custom.

I have heard that money corrupts people, and more money corrupts more. I personally observed this phenomenon in case of Mewawala. When Mewawala struggled to establish himself in the industry, he used to be a nice gentleman with very high moral values. He was humble, simple and a down to earth human being. The public issue helped him to collect substantial public money from the unsuspecting investors. He siphoned off large part of this money to his personal ventures and businesses. He also raised substantial loan from various financial institutions which were also diverted to other purposes. Rather than reviving the plant at Murbad, a new business venture was started abroad by one of his sons.

After siphoning off substantial money, the cylinder division was sold off, as the unit became sick. Many workmen were not paid their legitimate dues. The workers who sincerely worked for the company for many years were suddenly rendered jobless and the actual compensation which they were entitled was also not paid. Expo Gas Containers Limited which made remarkable progress at one point of time is reduced to a non-entity today. This pains me more than anyone else because; I toiled very hard for this company. This case is a typical example where one can sadly see, how easy it is for an industrialist in our country to plunder public money with impunity and escape from all scrutiny. I came to know that Mr. Mewawala died in a foreign country sometime in 2016. Some medical experts were of the opinion that my multiple myeloma could be due to the welding related fumes to which I was constantly exposed while working at the factory.

When I quit BIS I did not consult anyone and when I quit Expo Gas Containers Limited also I did not inform any of my close relatives. I also did not have any job, since I resigned without any plan and did not know what I would do further.

While I was in Expo Gas Containers Limited, I did the lead assessors course in ISO: 9001 -1995 International Standard for implementing Quality Management System (QMS) in an organization. After undergoing this training, I implemented the system in the company without any external assistance. This gave me the knowledge and the experience in implementing QMS in an organization. By now I was totally frustrated with the concept of working in any organization under some one. By this time I had also gained more than 17 years of varied industrial experience at various levels. I decided to be my own boss and work for myself with abundant freedom and for a purpose. I decided to become a freelance technical consultant. This was in July 1999.

My Ex-BIS colleagues Bagchi and Ashok Jadhav had taken up consultancy assignments for some companies in Mumbai. Since they officially worked with BIS, they were in search of a person through whom they could outsource the work. They offered me some assignments involving implementation of ISO: 9001 in some organizations. Few organizations where I provided consultancy services were- Dr. Batra's Homeopathy Clinic – India's leading homeopathy clinic, Allied Digital Services- a successful Indian MNC today, and Ceramco Dental Clinic- Andheri.

I was uncomfortable working under my ex- colleagues and there were disputes in sharing the consultancy fees. By this time I had also developed confidence and belief in my capability. I decided to be independent and started my own consultancy firm 'Quality Management & Technical Consultants' in October 1999. Initially Bagchi was upset with my decision, but later supported me whole heartedly.

Soon I started getting several consultancy assignments through the word of mouth publicity. I also implemented the system to near possible perfection and the firms were also happy with my quality of work and the services rendered to them.

My biggest break came, when I bagged the much sought after consultancy assignment of Punjab National Bank. The assignment was to train and implement ISO: 9001 Quality Management Systems in 30 branches of the bank, spread all over the state of Maharashtra.

The above assignment gave a big boost to my career and I became a well known technical expert in the industry. I am indebted to Punjab National Bank for two reasons. One, it considerably enhanced my earning and professional visibility. The second significant outcome was, meeting Dr. Vijayaragavan, manager of one of the branches in Nagpur. Subsequently we became very close family friends. Dr. Vijayaragavan was instrumental in diverting my career into teaching. My family members and I will ever remember Dr. Vijayaragavan for the good things he has done to us.

In April 2004, I changed the name of my proprietor firm to CKS Associates, as I was known in the industry by my initials- C K Sreedharan. I also became a panel auditor in one of the world's reputed systems certification bodies- Det Norske Veritas popularly known as DNV. It was a great honour and a symbol of recognition for my technical expertise. DNV had assorted distinguished technical experts from a wide spectrum of industry background.

As a part of the DNV audit team, I had opportunity to conduct audits in several reputed establishments like- Mumbai Port Trust, JNPT, L & T, Suzlon Industries, Kilburn Engineering, WMI Cranes, and many more. It was Prakash Tikare of DNV who was responsible for inducting me into the panel and I will ever remain grateful to him. As a DNV panel auditor, I was involved in more than 300 system audits of various companies during the period 2004 to 2008.

My consultancy work gave me an opportunity to closely work with other certification agencies like BVIS, SGS, BSI, BIS, TUV and many more. My overall assessment was- DNV auditors were the best, most professional, competent, and high on integrity – compared to the auditors from all other certification agencies. I am really proud that I had worked with such an esteemed organization for some time.

Boost your immune system naturally:

What you eat, your attitude, and the amount of exercise you get, can all play a role in strengthening your immune system and preventing illness. Laughter can boost your immune system along with your mood. It raises levels of antibodies in the blood and those of the white blood cells that attack and kill bacteria and viruses. It also increases the number of antibodies in the mucus made in the nose and respiratory passages.

A study of a German choir revealed that singing activates the spleen, helping to increase the blood concentrations of antibodies and boost the immune system.

Your immune system responds to exercise by producing more of the blood cells that attack bacterial invaders. And the more regularly you exercise, the more long-lasting the changes become.

(Source: Bombay Times, Mumbai edition dated 16 November, 2017)

Most tumours never make it beyond the microscopic stage; they disappear before we have a chance to know they exist, according to W. John Diamond, M.D. In the language of orthodox oncology, these tumours 'spontaneously regress.' The obvious implication, says Dr. Diamond, is that certain immune system components stop cancer in its tracks.

Patients with a variety of cancers often have decreased natural killer (NK) cell activity. The level of immune function, as measured by the activity of NK cells, has also been found to correlate with the spread of cancer in breast cancer patients. The length of time a cancer patient can be expected to live is directly related to levels of NK activity.

It has been estimated that approximately 300 cancer cells are produced daily by a healthy human body. 'Everybody produces cancer cells,' says Jesse Stoff, MD. 'It's the job of the immune system to look for these cells and destroy them.' In general, these cancer cells become a health issue under one of the following conditions:

1) There is an increased production of cancer cells due to the effect of cancer-causing substances. Individuals whose immune systems have been suppressed by drugs, radiation, or inherited disorder have cancer death rates 100 times that of the normal population.

2) There is decreased cancer-cell removal due to clogged lymph drainage.

3) The immune system is too depressed. 'The only time that somebody could actually develop a cancer is if the immune system is not on-guard,' says Dr. Stoff. If it is very sluggish in its duty of looking for these cells, cancer cells begin to accumulate into something large enough to be called a 'mass' and this can, of course, have deadly implications.

- W Lee Cowden- 'Longevity- An Alternative Medicine Definitive Guide.'

The diagnosis

'Fear keeps us focussed on the past or worried about the future. If we can acknowledge our fear, we can realize that right now we are okay. Right now, today, we are still alive.'

- Thich Nhat Hanh

Life as a consultant was very busy and hectic. I had to travel extensively to far- off places like Boisar, Palghar, Nasik, Madgaon, Pune etc on a regular basis. The work load was very erratic and unpredictable. Some months there was hectic work load and some other months there was hardly any work. I earned decent money and I really enjoyed my profession. I am also blessed in one major aspect. My wife is always happy with whatever I earn. She is content with our simple life style. My daughters also did not demand any great things. I was also not keen on making a lot of money. Hence there was no pressure on me to earn big money.

From the beginning of the year 2008, the good things slowly started disappearing, and my life drastically changed for the worst.

From January 2008, I started feeling neck pain and after some days I found it difficult to turn my head. I thought that I had developed temporary stiff neck due to wrong sleeping posture. I ignored the pain, hoping that it would go away on its own after a few days. I applied muscle relaxant sprays and tried general medications. I did not take the pain seriously. Right from my childhood I enjoyed disease free excellent health with hardly any major ailment. Once in a while I used to suffer from cough and cold and on rare occasions suffered a bout of fever lasting for a few days. I exercised regularly and had healthy eating habits. I had a great self belief that I was totally immune to all types of diseases.

Since the neck pain persisted for a long time, my wife and other family members pressurized me to seek medical advice. Under family compulsion, I reluctantly went to seek advice from my family doctor Vivek Bhosale, an experienced general physician, practicing in Kalyan. The doctor prescribed some medicines, mainly pain killers for about a week. I took the medicines as prescribed, but there was no relief. I didn't go for further consultation as advised by the doctor.

Holy, the festival of colour was on 21-03-20008. I can never forget this day. This day was the beginning of the distress not only for me but also for my entire family- my wife and my two daughters.

I owned a flat in 'Ákshata Apartment' in Kalyan. The residents followed the tradition of celebrating the festival by applying colours and playing with water. We all celebrated the festival and had fun in the building terrace. While throwing water on others, I felt as if one of my bones in my spinal cord, breaking with a clear sound. Immediately my whole body was paralyzed, and I could not move any part of my body. I felt a terrible stinging pain in my back. My wife with the assistance of my daughters brought me down to our flat. I laid down on the bed, unable to move my body.

Since it was a festival day my family doctor was not available for consultation. By evening my condition slightly improved, and my wife took me to another general physician. The doctor gave a pain killer injection and advised me to go for further investigations if my condition did not improve.

The pain persisted and while sleeping I found it extremely painful to shift from one side to another. By now I was a little bit worried. I consulted Dr. Vivek Bhosale, my family doctor. The doctor advised me to go for a x-ray examination of my spinal cord. I took a x-ray of my spinal cord. The film revealed some kind of fracture in one or two places of my spinal cord. The doctor was alarmed by now and he advised me to go for a MRI examination of the entire spinal cord region.

I took a MRI scan in Kalyan Scan Centre on 16.04.2008. MRI films revealed 'metastasis' or myeloid disorder. I did not understand anything from the report.

The next day I took the MRI report to Dr. Vivek Bhosale and he referred me to an orthopedic specialist in Shree Hospital, Kalyan. The specialist cautioned me that my problem could be serious and advised me to immediately consult an expert in Hinduja Hospital, Mumbai.

The scanned copy of the MRI report reference number 11004, dated 16-04-2008 is attached in the next page.

KALYAN SCAN CENTRE

OPEN MRI & WHOLE BODY CT SCAN CENTRE

Tel.: 2326326
2329618
2328765

REF NO : 110.04 DATE : 16/04/2008

PATIENT'S NAME : MR. C. K. SHRIDHARAN AGE : 50/M

REFERRED DOCTOR : DR. VIVEK BHOSALE

EXAMINATION : LIMITED MRI OF DORSAL SPINE

A plain MR of the dorsal spine was performed using T1 and T2 weighted sequences.

There is marked wedge compression of D6 vertebral body with compression of the thecal sac and indentation of cord surface, causing focal kyphotic deformity. There is mild stranding of the pre and paravertebral soft tissues.

All the cervical vertebral bodies and many of the spinous processes show diffuse hypointense signal on T1W images and patchy hyperintense signal on T2W images. Focal hyperintense areas are seen in D7 and D8 vertebral bodies.

There is diffuse disc bulge at D2-3 level, compressing the thecal sac. Rest of the intervertebral discs are normal.

There is no intraspinal / cystic space occupying lesion. Spinal cord reveals normal signal intensity, without any evidence of a focal lesion.

Screening sagittal sequences through the cervical spine reveals posterior disc protrusion at C6-7 level, compressing the thecal sac and indenting the cord. Mild disc bulges are seen at C4-5 and C5-6 levels, indenting the thecal sac. Bilateral uncovertebral osteophytes are noted between C3-4 and C5-6 levels. Almost all cervical vertebrae show patchy areas of hyperintense signal on T2W images.

Screening sagittal sequences through the lumbar spine reveals transitional vertebra at L5 level. All lumbar vertebrae show patchy hyperintense signal on T2W images. There is expansion of the left superior articular process of L2 vertebra and left inferior articular process of L1 vertebra. Diffuse disc bulges are seen at L3-4 and L4-5 levels, indenting the thecal sac.

ORGANISED BY : KALYAN CT SCAN CENTRE

7-10, SHREE KRISHNA APT., NEAR KARNIK ROAD, MURBAD ROAD, KALYAN 421 301.

KALYAN SCAN CENTRE

OPEN MRI & WHOLE BODY CT SCAN CENTRE

Tel.: 2326326
2329616
2328765

REMARKS :   Marked wedge compression of D6 vertebral body with compression of the thecal sac and indentation of cord surface, causing focal kyphotic deformity. Mild stranding of the pre and paravertebral soft tissues.

All the visualised vertebral bodies and many of the spinous processes show patchy hyperintense signal on T2W images with focal hyperintense areas in D7 and D8 vertebral bodies. Expansion of the left superior articular process of L2 vertebra and left inferior articular process of L1 vertebra.

The above imaging findings most likely represent neoplastic pathology – metastasis or myeloid disorder. Bone marrow biopsy is recommended for further evaluation.

Thanks for the Referral,
With Regards,

DR. ANUJA S. DESHPANDE
DMRD., DNB.

ORGANISED BY : KALYAN CT SCAN CENTRE

7-10, SHREE KRISHNA APT., NEAR KARNIK ROAD, MURBAD ROAD, KALYAN 421 301.

At that time, my elder brother was working with ONGC Panvel, and he referred my case to Dr. Meena Biswal, the resident doctor of ONGC. The doctor advised us to consult Dr. Abhey Nene, a renowned spine specialist in Hinduja. Dr. Abhey Nene was a most sought after doctor and I could not get his immediate appointment. Dr. Meena Biswal somehow managed to get his appointment at Hinduja Hospital on 18.04.2008.

On 18.04.2008, accompanied by my wife, brother and my brother-in-law, I consulted Dr. Abhey Nene at the Hinduja Hospital. The doctor advised that I had to undergo a series of tests and investigations to identify the actual problem and for that to happen, I should get admitted immediately. All my near and dear ones who accompanied me realized the gravity of the situation and advised me to follow the doctor's advice. Dr. Abhey Nene immediately checked for availability of bed in the hospital. A bed was available on 20.04.2008. Dr. Abhey Nene immediately booked the bed on my behalf, without waiting for our consent, as my case seemed to be a serious one. Once my consent was given, my blood sample was taken for carrying out various tests.

Only now the seriousness of my condition dawned on me and the developments hit me like a thunderbolt. All along I was just thinking that I just had some calcium deficiency, and that weakened my bone and it was a simple case of treating with calcium supplements.

I was devastated when I came to know from the doctor that my problem could be due to tuberculosis or multiple myeloma- a type of blood cancer. I was mainly concerned with the cost of treatment, which was quite high at Hinduja. I preached and advised everyone to take a medical insurance cover for the entire family at any cost. On a couple of occasions I almost completed the formalities for mediclaim, but did not complete the process due to some reason or the other. I didn't have any medical insurance cover when I required treatment for one of the most expensive diseases to medically treat. This was the third biggest blunder I committed in my life.

I was not financially sound to take up an expensive treatment, especially in a sophisticated multi-speciality hospital like Hinduja. I had some savings in my PPF account, and fortunately for me, it was awaiting renewal after completion of twenty years. I decided to close the account and use the proceeds for my treatment. My parents helped me with some contribution. My brother, brother-in-law and sisters willingly came forward to support me financially.

I got myself admitted into Hinduja Hospital on 20/04/2008. My brother accompanied me to the hospital and helped me in the admission process. I was admitted in the new building of Hinduja. My brother stayed with me for the first two days.

The next one week was very hectic for me. The hospital carried out a series of tests with excellent planning and coordination. I was quickly transported from one department to another department with clockwork precision. Several blood related tests, X-ray of entire body, C T guided biopsy, bone marrow interpretation, and several other tests were carried out. A sample of bone marrow was sent to Tata Memorial Hospital, Parel for molecular cytogenetics (Fish) report.

Dr. Abhey Nene and Dr. Sachin Almel carefully went through the test reports. Initially, the doctors could not precisely diagnose my disease as test results were not conclusive in some of the examinations. A PET scan was suggested to explore further, but it was dropped subsequently. Finally I was diagnosed as suffering from multiple myeloma with D 6 wedge compression. I came under the treatment of Dr. Sachin V Almel, MD., DM (Oncology).

Scanned copies of the reports of important tests carried out to diagnose my case are reproduced in the following pages as per the date of test. The reports are self explanatory.

Every day 1500 people die of cancer in India, making it the second most common cause of death in India after cardiovascular disease. And nearly 2000 new cancer cases are detected in the country daily according to National Institute of Cancer Prevention and Research. Projections put the number of new cases by 2020 at 17.3 lakh.

Environmental and lifestyle are among the leading risks. The incidence of lung cancer is registering a rise in metros, be it Bangalore or Delhi. Women in urban India are more likely to get breast cancer than those in rural areas.

In Bengaluru and Chennai more than quarter of the total number of cancers in women are of the breast. Mass screening is most important to detect cancer early.

(Source: Times of India, Mumbai edition dated 19 January, 2018)

P. D. HINDUJA NATIONAL HOSPITAL
& MEDICAL RESEARCH CENTRE
(Established and managed by the National Health & Education Society)

VEER SAVARKAR MARG, MAHIM, MUMBAI - 400 016, INDIA
PHONE : 2445 1515, 2445 2222, 2444 9199 FAX : 2444 9151

DEPARTMENT OF LABORATORY MEDICINE
HEMATOLOGY

ORDER NO. : 10932899

HH NO. : 1000298   ADM. NO. :

NAME : C K SREEDHARAN   AGE   50 YEARS   SEX   : MALE

DATE : 18/04/2008   LOCATION : OPD   REFERRED BY DR.   : NENE ABHAY M

Samp. Coll Dt : 18/04/2008 06:19:58PM   WorkSht.DtTm: 18/04/2008 06:29:08PM

CBC & ESR

Test	Result	Units	Abnormality	Reference Range
ESR	34.00	mm/hr	H	0.00 - 10.00
RED CELL COUNT	3.82	10^12/l	L	4.50 - 6.50
HEMOGLOBIN	11.40	g/dl	L	13.00 - 18.00
HEMATOCRIT	34.20	%	L	40.00 - 54.00
MCV	89.50	fl		76.00 - 96.00
MCH	29.80	pg		27.00 - 32.00
MCHC	33.30	g/dl		30.00 - 35.00
RDW	13.90	%		11.50 - 14.50
PLATELET COUNT	283.00	10^9/l		150.00 - 400.00
MPV	9.40	fl		6.80 - 12.60
WBC & DIFF COUNT				
WBC Count	6.97	10^9/l		4.00 - 11.00
Diff. WBC Count				
Neutrophils	54.00	%		40.00 - 75.00
Eosinophils	0.00	%	L	1.00 - 6.00
Lymphocytes	34.00	%		20.00 - 45.00
Monocytes	12.00	%	H	2.00 - 10.00
Basophils	0.00	%		0.00 - 1.00

DR. S.KHODAIJI / DR. A. S. DESHPANDE
Consultant, Hematologist
Report Printed On :   18-Apr-2008 23:44

P. D. HINDUJA NATIONAL HOSPITAL
& MEDICAL RESEARCH CENTRE
(Established and managed by the National Health & Education Society)

VEER SAVARKAR MARG, MAHIM, MUMBAI - 400 016, INDIA
PHONE : 2445 1515, 2445 2222; 2444 9199 FAX : 2444 9151

DEPARTMENT OF LABORATORY MEDICINE
BIOCHEMISTRY

ORDER NO. : 10932899

HH NO. : 1000298   ADM. NO.

NAME   : C K SREEDHARAN

AGE   : 50 YEARS   SEX   : MALE

DATE   : 18/04/2008   LOCATION   : OPD

REFERRED BY DR.   : NENE ABHAY M

Samp. Coll Dt   18/04/2008 06:19:58PM

WorkSht.DtTm   18/04/2008 06:29:08PM

Main Lab

SERUM ELECTROPHORESIS

Test	Result	Units	Status	Reference Range	
Total Protein	7.40	g/dl		6.70 -	8.20
Albumin	4.20	g/dl		3.50 -	5.00
Globulin	3.20	g/dl		2.60 -	4.10
A/G Ratio	1.30			1.20 -	2.50
ELECTROPHORESIS					
Alpha - 1 Globulins	0.20	g dl		0.10 -	0.40
Alpha - 2 Globulins	0.90	g/dl		0.40 -	1.20
Beta Globulins	1.20	g/dl	H	0.50 -	1.10
Gamma Globulins	0.90	g/dl		0.50 -	1.60

Comments :   Protein electrophoresis within normal limits.

* * End of Report * *

21/4/08

DR. T. F. ASHAVAID

Consultant Biochemist
Report Printed On :   21-Apr-2008 17:40

P. D. HINDUJA NATIONAL HOSPITAL
& MEDICAL RESEARCH CENTRE
(Established and managed by the National Health & Education Society)

VEER SAVARKAR MARG, MAHIM, MUMBAI - 400 016, INDIA
PHONE : 2445 1515, 2445 2222, 2444 9199 FAX : 2444 9151

DEPARTMENT OF LABORATORY MEDICINE
HEMATOLOGY

ORDER NO. : 10933166   HH NO. : 1000298   ADM. NO. :

NAME   : C K SREEDHARAN   AGE   : 50 YEARS   SEX   : MALE

DATE   : 18/04/2008   LOCATION   : OPD   REFERRED BY DR   : NENE ABHAY M

Samp. Coll Dt : 18/04/2008 07:29:53PM   WorkSht.DtTm: 18/04/2008 07:50:13PM

Test	Result	Units	Abnormality	Reference Range
PROTHROMBIN TIME				
Patient	10.40	sec		7.60 - 10.60
Mean Normal	9.70	sec		7.60 - 10.60
INR	1.07			

* * End of Report * *

DR. S.KHODAIJI / DR. A. S. DESHPANDE
Consultant, Hematologist
Report Printed On :   19-Apr-2008 05:55

46

P. D. HINDUJA NATIONAL HOSPITAL
& MEDICAL RESEARCH CENTRE
(Established and managed by the National Health & Education Society)

VEER, SAVARKAR MARG, MAHIM, MUMBAI - 400 016, INDIA
PHONE : 2445 1515, 2445 2222, 2444 9199 FAX : 2444 9151

DEPARTMENT OF LABORATORY MEDICINE

BLOOD BANK

ORDER NO.   :   10932899   HH NO. :   : 1000298   ADM. NO. :

NAME   :   C K SREEDHARAN   AGE   : 50 YEARS   SEX   : MALE

DATE   : 18/04/2008   LOCATION : : OPD   REFERRED BY   : DR. NENE ABHAY M

Test	Results
HIV ANTIGEN & ANTIBODY (I &II) (MEIA)	NEGATIVE

MEIA - Microparticle Enzyme Immunoassay

DR.A.S.DESHPANDE / DR. S. KHODAIJI
Consultant Transfusion Medicine & Hematology

Report Printed On : 19-Apr-2008 12:13

P. D. HINDUJA NATIONAL HOSPITAL
& MEDICAL RESEARCH CENTRE
(Established and managed by the National Health & Education Society)

VEER SAVARKAR MARG, MAHIM, MUMBAI - 400 016, INDIA
PHONE : 2445 1515, 2445 2222, 2444 9199 FAX : 2444 9151

DEPARTMENT OF LABORATORY MEDICINE
HEMATOLOGY

ORDER NO. : 10932699

HH NO. : 1000298   ADM. NO. :

NAME   : C K SREEDHARAN

AGE : 50 YEARS   SEX   : MALE

DATE · 18/04/2008   LOCATION : OPD

REFERRED BY DR. : NENE ABHAY M

Samp. Coll Dt : 18/04/2008 06:19:58PM

WorkSht.DtTm: 18/04/2008 06:29:08PM

BLEEDING & CLOTTING TIME

Test	Result	Units	Status	Reference Range
BLEEDING TIME (DUKE 'S METHOD)	2.05	min		2.00 - 6.00
CLOTTING TIME	4.07	min		2.00 - 7.00

* * End of Report * *

DR. S.KHODAIJI / DR. A. S. DESHPANDE
Consultant, Hematologist
Report Printed On :   18-Apr-2008 20:04

P. D. HINDUJA ..ATIONAL HOSPITAL
& MEDICAL RESEARCH CENTRE
(Established and managed by the National Health & Education Society)

VEER SAVARKAR MARG, MAHIM, MUMBAI - 400 016, INDIA
PHONE : 2445 1515, 2445 2222, 2444 9199 FAX : 2444 9151

DEPARTMENT OF LABORATORY MEDICINE
BIOCHEMISTRY

ORDER NO. : 10939070	HH NO. : 1000298	ADM. NO. : 1076642
NAME : C K SREEDHARAN	AGE : 50 YEARS	SEX : MALE
DATE : 20/04/2008 LOCATION : 21S3	REFERRED BY DR. : NENE ABHAY M	
Samp. Coll Dt 20/04/2008 06:34:07PM	WorkSht.DtTm	20/04/2008 06:47:50PM
Stat Lab		

GENERAL BODY PROFILE

Test		Result	Units	Status	Reference Range
Random Blood Glucose	Conventional	93.00	mg/dl		
	S.I.	5.12	mmol/l		
Sodium	Conventional	138.70	mEq /l		135.00 - 147.0
	S.I.	138.70	mmol/l		135.00 - 147.00
Potassium	Conventional	4.05	mEq/l		3.30 - 4.80
	S.I.	4.05	mmol/l		3.30 - 4.80
Chloride	Conventional	107.10	mEq/l		101.00 - 111.0
	S.I.	107.10	mmol/l		101.00 - 111.00
TCO2	Conventional	28.20	mmol/l	H	23.00 - 27.00
	S.I.	28.20	mmol/l		23.00 - 27.00
Anion Gap	Conventional	7.40	mEq/l	L	8.00 - 12.00
	S.I.	7.40	mmol/l		8.00 - 12.00
Blood Urea Nitrogen	Conventional	15.00	mg/dl		5.00 - 25.00
	S.I.	5.36	mmol/l		1.79 - 8.93
Osmolality (calculated)		277.50	mOsm/l	L	280.00 - 295.00
Creatinine	Conventional	0.90	mg/dl		0.60 - 1.10
	S.I.	79.56	umol/l		53.04 - 97.24

DR. T. F. ASHAVAID

Consultant Biochemist
Report Printed On :   20-Apr-2008 19:40

P. D. HINDUJA ATIONAL HOSPITAL
& MEDICAL RESEARCH CENTRE
(Established and managed by the National Health & Education Society)

VEER SAVARKAR MARG, MAHIM, MUMBAI - 400 016, INDIA
PHONE : 2445 1515, 2445 2222, 2444 9199 FAX : 2444 9151

DEPARTMENT OF LABORATORY MEDICINE
BIOCHEMISTRY

ORDER NO. : 10939070   HH NO. : 1000296   ADM. NO. : 1076842

NAME   : C K SREEDHARAN   AGE   : 50 YEARS   SEX   : MALE

DATE   : 20/04/2008   LOCATION : 21S3   REFERRED BY DR.   : NENE ABHAY M

Samp. Coll Dt   20/04/2008 06:34 07PM   WorkSht.DtTm   20/04/2008 06:47:50PM

Stat Lab

GENERAL BODY PROFILE

Test		Result	Units	Status	Reference Range	
Calcium	Conventional	9.20	mg/dl		8.00 -	10.40
	S.I.	2.30	mmol/l		2.00 -	2.60
Total Protein	Conventional	6.80	g/dl		6.70 -	8.20
	S.I.	68.00	g/l		67.00 -	82.00
Albumin	Conventional	4.30	g/dl		3.50 -	5.00
	S.I.	43.00	g/l		35.00 -	50.00
Globulin	Conventional	2.50	g/dl	L	2.50 -	4.10
	S.I.	25.00	g/l		26.00 -	41.00
A/G Ratio		1.70			1.20 -	2.50
Bilirubin(Total)	Conventional	0.60	mg/dl		0.20 -	1.00
	S.I.	10.26	umol/l		3.42 -	17.10
SGOT	Conventional	13.00	U/l	L	15.00 -	48.00
	S.I.	13.00	IU/l		15.00 -	48.00
SGPT	Conventional	14.00	U/l		10.00 -	40.00
	S.I.	14.00	IU/l		10.00 -	40.00
Alkaline Phosphatase	Conventional	69.00	U/l		40.00 -	120.0
	S.I.	69.00	IU/l		40.00 -	120.00

DR. T. F. ASHAVAID

Consultant Biochemist
Report Printed On :   20-Apr-2008 19:40

P. D. HINDUJA ..ATIONAL HOSPITAL
& MEDICAL RESEARCH CENTRE
(Established and managed by the National Health & Education Society)

VEER SAVARKAR MARG, MAHIM, MUMBAI - 400 016, INDIA
PHONE : 2445 1515, 2445 2222, 2444 9199 FAX : 2444 9151

DEPARTMENT OF LABORATORY MEDICINE

BIOCHEMISTRY

ORDER NO. : 10939070 HH NO. : 1000298 ADM. NO : 1076842

NAME : C K SREEDHARAN AGE : 50 YEARS SEX : MALE

DATE : 20/04/2008 LOCATION : 21S3 REFERRED BY DR. : NENE ABHAY M

Samp. Coll Dt 20/04/2008 06.34.07PM WorkSht.Dt:Tm 20/04/2008 06:47:50PM

Stat Lab

GENERAL BODY PROFILE

Test		Result	Units	Status	Reference Range
Gamma G.T.	Conventional	20.00	U/I		0.00 - 60.00
	S.I.	20.00	IU/l		0.00 - 60.00

* * End of Report * *

DR. T.-F. ASHAVAID

Consultant Biochemist
Report Printed On : 20-Apr-2008 19:40

P. D. HINDUJA NATIONAL HOSPITAL
& MEDICAL RESEARCH CENTRE
(Established and managed by the National Health & Education Society)

VEER SAVARKAR MARG, MAHIM, MUMBAI - 400 016, INDIA
PHONE : 2445 1515, 2445 2222, 2444 9199 FAX : 2444 9151

DEPARTMENT OF IMAGING

NAME	: C K SREEDHARAN	AGE	: 50 YEARS	SEX	: MALE
HH NO.	: 1000298	LOCATION : 21S3	ADM NO. : 1076842	EXAM NO. : 8814	
REFERRED BY	: DR. NENE ABHAY M		ORDER NO. : 10939070	DATE	: 20/04/2008

EXAMINATION
X-RAY CHEST PA

REPORT DETAILS

High KV frontal chest radiograph shows normal soft tissues and bony cage.

The cardiac size is within normal limits and the cardiac silhoutte is normal.

Both lung fields are clear. The pleural spaces are clear. No hilar,

diaphragmatic or mediastinal lesion is seen.

CONCLUSION :- NORMAL X - RAY OF CHEST.

DR. J.M. MODHE - M.D.
CONSULTANT - RADIOLOGIST
sd
21.04.2008

Report printed on : 21/04/2008 10:26 AM
Page 1 of 1

P. D. HINDUJA NATIONAL HOSPITAL
& MEDICAL RESEARCH CENTRE
(Established and managed by the National Health & Education Society)

VEER SAVARKAR MARG, MAHIM, MUMBAI - 400 016, INDIA
PHONE : 2445 1515, 2445 2222, 2444 9199 FAX : 2444 9151

DEPARTMENT OF LABORATORY MEDICINE

BLOOD BANK

ORDER NO : 10939070   HH NO. : : 1000298   ADM. NO : 1076842

NAME   : C K SREEDHARAN   AGE   : 50 YEARS   SEX   : MALE

DATE   : 20/04/2008   LOCATION : : 21S3   REFERRED BY   : DR. NENE ABHAY M

Test	Results
HEPATITIS B (HBsAg) (MEIA)	NEGATIVE
HCV ANTIBODY (MEIA)	NEGATIVE

MEIA - Microparticle Enzyme Immunoassay

DR.A.S.DESHPANDE / DR. S. KHODAIJI
Consultant Transfusion Medicine & Hematology

Report Printed On : 21-Apr-2008 14:51

53

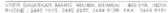

P. D. HINDUJA NATIONAL HOSPITAL
& MEDICAL RESEARCH CENTRE
(Established and managed by the National Health & Education Society)

VEER SAVARKAR MARG, MAHIM, MUMBAI - 400 016, INDIA
PHONE : 2445 1515, 2445 2222, 2444 9199 FAX : 2444 9151

DEPARTMENT OF LABORATORY MEDICINE
HEMATOLOGY

ORDER NO. : 10939124	HH NO. : 1000298	ADM. NO. : 1076842	
NAME : C K SREEDHARAN	AGE : 50 YEARS	SEX : MALE	
DATE : 20/04/2008 LOCATION : 21S3	REFERRED BY DR. NENE ABHAY M		
Samp. Coll Dt : 20/04/2008 08:35:24PM	WorkSht.DtTm: 20/04/2008 06:47:15PM		

Test	Result	Units	Abnormality	Reference Range
ACTIVATED PARTIAL THROMBOPLASTIN TIME				
Patient	29.00	sec		22.70 - 33.30
Control	30.80	sec		22.70 - 33.30

* * End of Report * *

DR. S.KHODAIJI / DR. A. S. DESHPANDE
Consultant, Hematologist
Report Printed On : 20-Apr-2008 19:29

Probiotics help to keep diseases at bay:

These are live bacteria that are essential to keep the gut healthy and are often known as 'good' or 'helpful bacteria.' Probiotics create a protective layer, which helps in keeping diseases at bay.

They are helpful in improving digestion and immunity. They reduce the chances of developing diseases such as cancer.

Probiotics are not a one-time medicine that can deliver immediate results; however, long-term intake is sure to give strong benefits.

P. D. HINDUJA ___ TIONAL HOSPITAL
& MEDICAL RESEARCH CENTRE
(Established and managed by the National Health & Education Society)

VEER SAVARKAR MARG, MAHIM, MUMBAI - 400 016, INDIA
PHONE : 2445 1515, 2445 2222, 2444 9199 FAX : 2444 9151

DEPARTMENT OF LABORATORY MEDICINE

HISTOPATHOLOGY

VOUCHER NO : 10943370	HH NO. : 1000298	ADM NO : 1076842
NAME : C K SREEDHARAN	AGE : 50 Yrs	SEX : Male
REFERRED BY : NENE ABHAY M	LOC. : 21S3	DATE : 21/04/2008 04:39

SAMP.COLL.DTTM: 21/04/2008 04:39:48 PM　　WORKSHT.DTTM: 21/04/2008 04:46:33 PM

S-1974/08

CT GUIDED BIOPSY - D6 VERTEBRAL LESION :

CLINICAL HISTORY : C/o Back pain.
MRI - S/o D6 collapse ? Neoplasm 　? Infective 　? TB.

GROSS :

Received three linear haemorrhagic cores ranging from 0.2cm to 6cm long. (? Clot).

MICROSCOPY :

Sections show sheets of uniformly packed minimally atypical plasma cells. In many paces, the plasma cells are in cords with thin colloid capillary vessels. There is intralesional haemorrhage with scattered lymphocytes and neutrophils.

DIAGNOSIS :

CT GUIDED BIOPSY - D6 VERTEBRAL LESION :
PLASMACYTOMA.
ADVISED SKELETAL SURVEY AND SERUM IMMUNOELECTROPHORESIS FOR 'M' BAND.

--End of report--

DR.R.B.DESHPANDE
MD
Consultant Histopathologist

DR. ANITA S. BHADURI
MD
Consultant Histopathologist

Report Printed On : 24/04/2008 12:59:01　　Authenticated On : 24/04/2008 12:59:00

P. D. HINDUJA NATIONAL HOSPITAL
& MEDICAL RESEARCH CENTRE
(Established and managed by the National Health & Education Society)

VEER SAVARKAR MARG, MAHIM, MUMBAI - 400 016, INDIA
PHONE : 2445 1515, 2445 2222, 2444 9199 FAX : 2444 9151

DEPARTMENT OF LABORATORY MEDICINE : MICROBIOLOGY

ORDER NO : 10943370   HH NO : 1000298   ADMNNO : 1076842

NAME : C K SREEDHARAN   AGE : 50 Years   SEX : MALE

DATE : 21/04/2008 LOCATION : 21S3 REFERRED BY DR. NENE ABHAY M

CULTURE MISCELLANEOUS

SPECIMEN   VERTEBRAL BODY

GRAM STAIN(PRIMARY)
Pus Cells   OCCASIONAL
Organisms   NOT APPARENT

ZIEHL NIELSON STAIN (AFB)
Acid Fast Bacilli   NOT SEEN
Culture Aerobes   NO GROWTH

PLEASE AWAIT CULTURE TB MGIT REPORT.

DR. AJITA MEHTA / DR. CAMILLA RODRIGUES
MD,DPB   MD

Consultant Microbiologist

Report Printed On   23-Apr-2008 11:37

P. D. HINDUJA NATIONAL HOSPITAL
& MEDICAL RESEARCH CENTRE
(Established and managed by the National Health & Education Society)

VEER SAVARKAR MARG, MAHIM, MUMBAI - 400 016, INDIA
PHONE : 2445 1515, 2445 2222, 2444 9199 FAX : 2444 9151

DEPARTMENT OF LABORATORY MEDICINE
MICROBIOLOGY

ORDER NO. : 10943370   HH NO. : 1000298   ADM. NO. : 1076842

NAME   : C K SREEDHARAN   AGE   : 50 YEARS   SEX   · MALE

DATE   : 21/04/2008   LOCATION   : 21S3   REFERRED BY DR.   : NENE ABHAY M

Samp. Coll Dt. 21/04/2008 04:39:48PM   WorkSht.DtTm: 21/04/2008 04:46:33PM

CULTURE TB MGIT & IDENTIFICATION

Test	Result
Specimen	Vertibral Body Tissue
Acid Fast Bacilli	Not Seen
Conclusion	Await Culture TB MGIT report

Comments :   Bactec MGIT 960 TB system performed by rapid detection and continous monitoring using flourescence method.

Comments :   REFERENCE NUMBER : 2121
PLEASE QUOTE THIS TB MGIT REFERENCE NUMBER FOR FURTHER PROGRESS ON YOUR
REPORT.
3 WEEKS REPORT ON : 13/05/2008   (FROM OPD REPORT COUNTER)
6 WEEKS REPORT ON : 03/06/2008   (FROM OPD REPORT COUNTER)

* * End of Report * *

DR. AJITA MEHTA / DR. CAMILLA RODRIGUES
MD,DPB   MD

Consultant Microbiologist
Report Printed On :   22-Apr-2008 16:46

P. D. HINDUJA NATIONAL HOSPITAL
& MEDICAL RESEARCH CENTRE
(Established and managed by the National Health & Education Society)

VEER SAVARKAR MARG, MAHIM, MUMBAI - 400 016, INDIA
PHONE : 2445 1515, 2445 2222, 2444 9199 FAX : 2444 9151

DEPARTMENT OF LABORATORY MEDICINE
HEMATOLOGY

ORDER NO. : 10948649

HH NO. : 1000298   ADM. NO. : 1076842

NAME : C K SREEDHARAN

AGE : 50 YEARS   SEX : MALE

DATE : 22/04/2008   LOCATION :

REFERRED BY DR. : NENE ABHAY M

Samp. Coll Dt : 22/04/2008 12:12:49PM

WorkSht.DtTm: 22/04/2008 12:22:00PM

BONE MARROW INTERPRETATION

BM Smear No. :   118 / 08

Cellularity :   Hypercellular

M:E Ratio :   2.4 : 1

Erythropoiesis :   Reduced. Normoblastic.

Myelopoiesis :   Suppressed due to increased number of plasma cells

Lymphopoiesis :   Lymphocytes - 7%, Plasma cells - 60%. Immature and
                                binucleate plasma cells seen.

Megakaryopoiesis :   Megakaryocytes are adequate in number.

Impression :   Picture suggestive of multiple myeloma.

Comments : Advised : To correlate with clinical, biochemical and radiological findings.

* * End of Report * *

DR. S.KHODAIJI / DR A. S. DESHPANDE
Consultant, Hematologist
Report Printed On :   28-Apr-2008 16:35

P. D. HINDUJA NATIONAL HOSPITAL
& MEDICAL RESEARCH CENTRE
(Established and managed by the National Health & Education Society)

VEER, SAVARKAR, MARG, MAHIM, MUMBAI - 400 016, INDIA
PHONE : 2445 1515, 2445 2222, 2444 9199 FAX : 2444 9151

DEPARTMENT OF LABORATORY MEDICINE
BIOCHEMISTRY

ORDER NO. : 10947662

HH NO. : 1000296   ADM. NO. : 1976842

NAME   . C K SREEDHARAN   AGE   :   50 YEARS   SEX   : MALE

DATE   : 22/04/2008   LOCATION : 21S3   REFERRED BY DR.   : NENE ABHAY M

Samp. Coll Dt   22/04/2008 02:45:23PM   WorkSht.DtTm   22/04/2008 02:53.45PM

Main Lab

ENZYME IMMUNOASSAY FOR THE QUANTITATIVE MEASUREMENT OF CA-19 -9 IN HUMAN SERUM

Test	Result	Units	Status	Reference Range
CA-19-9	56.20	u/ml	H	2.00 - 37.00
Method : MEIA : Microparticle Enhanced Immunoassay				

* * End of Report * *

DR. T. F. ASHAVAID

Consultant Biochemist
Report Printed On :   23-Apr-2008 14:31

P. D. HINDUJA N..TIONAL HOSPITAL
& MEDICAL RESEARCH CENTRE
(Established and managed by the National Health & Education Society)

VEER SAVARKAR MARG, MAHIM, MUMBAI - 400 016, INDIA
PHONE : 2445 1515, 2445 2222, 2444 9199 FAX : 2444 9151

DEPARTMENT OF LABORATORY MEDICINE
R I A

ORDER NO.   :   10947662

NAME   : C K SREEDHARAN

DATE   : 22/04/2008   LOCATION   : 21S3

Samp. Coll Dt: 22/04/2008 02:45:23PM

HH NO. :   1000298   ADM NO. :   1076842

AGE   :   50 YEARS   SEX   : MALE

REFERRED BY DR.   : NENE ABHAY M

WorkSht.DtTm: 22/04/2008 02:53:45PM

Test	Result	Units	Status	Reference Range
Carcino Embryonic Antigen (CEA)	0.79	ng/ml	Smokers Non-Smokers	: Upto 5.2 : Upto 3.4

DR. VIPLA PURI

Consultant - RIA

Printed On :   23-Apr-2008 16:09

P. D. HINDUJA NATIONAL HOSPITAL
& MEDICAL RESEARCH CENTRE
(Established and managed by the National Health & Education Society)

VEER SAVARKAR MARG, MAHIM, MUMBAI - 400 016, INDIA
PHONE : 2445 1515, 2445 2222, 2444 9199 FAX : 2444 9151

DEPARTMENT OF LABORATORY MEDICINE

R I A

ORDER NO. : 10947662   HH NO. : 1000298   ADM. NO. : 1076642

NAME : C K SREEDHARAN   AGE : 60 YEARS   SEX : MALE

DATE : 22/04/2008   LOCATION : 21S3   REFERRED BY DR. : NENE ABHAY M

Samp. Coll Dt: 22/04/2008 02.45:23PM   WorkSht.DtTm: 22/04/2008 02:53:45PM

Test	Result	Units	Status	Reference Range
Human Chorionic Gonadotropin (HCG)	* < 1.0	mIU/ml		0.00 - 5.00

Comments : * Rechecked

* * End of Report * *

DR. VIPLA PURI

Consultant - RIA

Printed On :   23-Apr-2008 15:10

P. D. HINDUJA ..ATIONAL HOSPITAL
& MEDICAL RESEARCH CENTRE
(Established and managed by the National Health & Education Society)

VEER SAVARKAR MARG, MAHIM MUMBAI - 400 016, INDIA
PHONE : 2445 1515, 2445 2222, 2444 9199 FAX : 2444 9151

DEPARTMENT OF LABORATORY MEDICINE
BIOCHEMISTRY

ORDER NO.   :   10944974   HH NO. :   1000298   ADM. NO. :   1076842

NAME   : C K SREEDHARAN   AGE   :   50 YEARS   SEX   : MALE

DATE   : 22/04/2008   LOCATION   : 21S3   REFERRED BY DR.   : NENE ABHAY M

Samp. Coll Dt   22/04/2008 09:16:39AM   WorkSht.DtTm   22/04/2008 09:22:20AM

Main Lab

BENCE JONES PROTEINS (24HRS)

Test	Result	Units	Status	Reference Range
Urine Volume	1,600.00	ml/24hrs		
Bence Jones Proteins	ABSENT			

* * End of Report * *

DR. T. F. ASHAVAID

Consultant Biochemist
Report Printed On :   22-Apr-2008 17:50

P. D. HINDUJA NATIONAL HOSPITAL
& MEDICAL RESEARCH CENTRE
(Established and managed by the National Health & Education Society)

VEER SAVARKAR MARG, MAHIM, MUMBAI - 400 016, INDIA
PHONE : 2445 1515, 2445 2222, 2444 9199 FAX : 2444 9151

DEPARTMENT OF LABORATORY MEDICINE
R I A

ORDER NO. : 10947662		HH NO. : 1000298	ADM. NO. : 1076842
NAME : C K SREEDHARAN		AGE : 50 YEARS	SEX : MALE
DATE : 22/04/2008 LOCATION : 21S3		REFERRED BY DR. : NENE ABHAY M	

Samp. Coll Dt: 22/04/2008 02:45:23PM   WorkSht.DtTm: 22/04/2008 02:53:45PM

Test	Result	Units	Status	Reference Range
Alpha Feto Protein (AFP)	3.25	IU/ml		0.00 - 5.00

** End of Report **

DR. VIPLA PURI

Consultant - RIA

Printed On :   23-Apr-2008 15:09

P. D. HINDUJA NATIONAL HOSPITAL
& MEDICAL RESEARCH CENTRE
(Established and managed by the National Health & Education Society)

VEER SAVARKAR MARG, MAHIM, MUMBAI - 400 016, INDIA
PHONE : 2445 1515, 2445 2222, 2444 9199 FAX : 2444 9151

DEPARTMENT OF LABORATORY MEDICINE
R I A

ORDER NO.   :   10947662   HH NO. :   1000298   ADM. NO :   1076842

NAME   : C K SREEDHARAN   AGE   :   50 YEARS   SEX   : MALE

DATE   : 22/04/2008   LOCATION   : 21S3   REFERRED BY DR.   : NENE ABHAY M

Samp. Coll Dt: 22/04/2008 02:45.23PM   WorkSht.DtTm: 22/04/2008 02:53:45PM

Test	Result	Units	Status	Reference Range
Prostate Specific Antigen (PSA) (Third Generation)	0.72	ng/ml		0.00 - 2.80

DR. VIPLA PURI

Consultant - RIA
Printed On :   23-Apr-2008 15:09

P. D. HINDUJA NATIONAL HOSPITAL
& MEDICAL RESEARCH CENTRE
(Established and managed by the National Health & Education Society)

VEER SAVARKAR MARG, MAHIM, MUMBAI - 400 016, INDIA
PHONE : 2445 1515, 2445 2222, 2444 9199 FAX : 2444 9151

DEPARTMENT OF LABORATORY MEDICINE
BIOCHEMISTRY

ORDER NO. : 10954805	HH NO. : 1000298	ADM. NO. : 1076842	
NAME : C K SREEDHARAN	AGE : 50 YEARS	SEX : MALE	
DATE : 24/04/2008 LOCATION : 21S3	REFERRED BY DR. : NENE ABHAY M		
Samp. Coll Dt 24/04/2008 03:51:22AM	WorkSht.DtTm 24/04/2008 05:28:29AM		

Main Lab

SERUM IMMUNO FIXATION ELECTROPHORESIS (IFE)

Serum IFE does not show presence of any predominent light chain.

* * End of Report * *

DR. T. F. ASHAVAID

Consultant Biochemist
Report Printed On :   24-Apr-2008 17:32

P. D. HINDUJA NATIONAL HOSPITAL
& MEDICAL RESEARCH CENTRE
(Established and managed by the National Health & Education Society)

VEER SAVARKAR MARG, MAHIM, MUMBAI - 400 016, INDIA
PHONE : 2445 1515, 2445 2222, 2444 9199 FAX : 2444 9151

DEPARTMENT OF LABORATORY MEDICINE
BIOCHEMISTRY

ORDER NO. : 10954605   HH NO. : 1000298   ADM. NO. : 1076842

NAME : C K SREEDHARAN   AGE : 50 YEARS   SEX : MALE

DATE : 24/04/2008   LOCATION : 21S3   REFERRED BY DR. : NENE ABHAY M

Samp. Coll Dt 24/04/2008 03:51:22AM   WorkSht.DtTm   24/04/2008 05:28:29AM

Main Lab

Test		Result	Units	Status	Reference Range
LDH	Conventional	95.00	U/L	L	135.00 - 225.0
	S.I.	95.00	IU/I		135.00 - 225.00

** End of Report **

DR. T. F. ASHAVAID

Consultant Biochemist
Report Printed On :   24-Apr-2008 09:43

P. D. HINDUJA NATIONAL HOSPITAL
& MEDICAL RESEARCH CENTRE
(Established and managed by the National Health & Education Society)

VEER SAVARKAR MARG, MAHIM, MUMBAI - 400 016, INDIA
PHONE : 2445 1515, 2445 2222, 2444 9199 FAX : 2444 9151

DEPARTMENT OF LABORATORY MEDICINE
RIA

ORDER NO. : 10954805   HH NO. : 1000298   ADM. NO. : 1076842

NAME : C K SREEDHARAN   AGE : 50 YEARS   SEX : MALE

DATE : 24/04/2008   LOCATION : 21S3   REFERRED BY DR. : NENE ABHAY M

Samp. Coll Dt: 24/04/2008 03:51:22AM   WorkSht.DtTm: 24/04/2008 05:28:29AM

Test	Result	Units	Status	Reference Range
Beta 2 Microglobulin(B2M)	3485.0	ng/ml	H	609.00 - 2366.00

* * End of Report * *

DR. VIPLA PURI

Consultant - RIA
Printed On :   24-Apr-2008 14:29

67

P. D. HINDUJA NATIONAL HOSPITAL
& MEDICAL RESEARCH CENTRE
(Established and managed by the National Health & Education Society)

VEER SAVARKAR MARG, MAHIM, MUMBAI - 400 016, INDIA
PHONE : 2445 1515, 2445 2222, 2444 9199 FAX : 2444 9151

DEPARTMENT OF LABORATORY MEDICINE
BIOCHEMISTRY

ORDER NO : 10961470   HH NO. : 1000298   ADM. NO. : 1076842

NAME : C K SREEDHARAN   AGE : 50 YEARS   SEX : MALE

DATE : 25/04/2008   LOCATION :   REFERRED BY DR. : ALMEL SACHIN V

Samp. Coll Dt   25/04/2008 12:47:05PM   WorkSht.DtTm   25/04/2008 12:49:16PM

Main Lab

URINARY PROTEIN ELECTROPHORESIS

Urine protein electrophoresis shows presence of a faint band at 100 X concentration.

* * End of Report * *

DR. T. F. ASHAVAID

Consultant Biochemist
Report Printed On :   28-Apr-2008 14:53

P. D. HINDUJA NATIONAL HOSPITAL
& MEDICAL RESEARCH CENTRE
(Established and managed by the National Health & Education Society)

VEER SAVARKAR MARG, MAHIM, MUMBAI - 400 018, INDIA
PHONE : 2445 1515, 2445 2222, 2444 9199 FAX : 2444 9151

DEPARTMENT OF LABORATORY MEDICINE
BIOCHEMISTRY

ORDER NO.   :   10970009

HH NO :   1000298   ADM. NO. :   1076842

NAME   : C K SREEDHARAN

AGE   :   50 YEARS   SEX   : MALE

DATE   : 27/04/2008   LOCATION   .

REFERRED BY DR.   : ALMEL SACHIN V

Samp. Coll Dt   27/04/2008 01:10:55PM

WorkSht.DtTm   27/04/2008 01:11:26PM

Main Lab

URINARY IFE

Urine Immunofixation electrophoresis shows presence of Kappa light chain at 100 X concentration.

* * End of Report * *

DR. T. F. ASHAVAID

Consultant Biochemist

Report Printed On :   28-Apr-2008 14:55

69

TATA MEMORIAL HOSPITAL
Dr. Ernest Borges Marg, Parel, Mumbai-400 012, India.
Tel : 24177000, Extn:4369, Fax: 022-24146937
E-mail: cancercytogeneticstmh@vsnl.com

CANCER CYTOGENETICS LABORATORY

Case No. RG/13342   Requisition No. VZZ/FI/08/001315   Lab No. **CG1164/CD**

Name   Mr. C K SREEDHARAN   Phone No 0

Sex / Age   M.50   Category/Status F/ Out Patient   Fax   0

Referred By   HINDUJA HOSP   Req. Dt   24/04/2008

Clinical Details   At Diagnosis   Specimen Type Bone Marrow Aspiration

Clinico-Hematological Diagnosis   Specimen Status OK

MOLECULAR CYTOGENETICS (FISH) REPORT   09/05/2008

Method   : Direct Harvesting of Bone Marrow Aspirate/Peripheral Blood, Lymph Node
                  Fluorescence in situ hybridization on interphase and metaphase cells
                  Ploidy Analysis by Chromosome Counting

Test   : t(4;14),t(11;14) and IgH translocation analysis

Probes/Probe panel : Vysis Inc. locus specific IGH/FGF3 & IGH/MYEOV dual (reciprocal) fusion
                  translocation probe &. Vysis Inc. locus specific IgH (14q32) dual colour break apart
                  rearrangement probe

Number of Cells Analyzed : 200

Result   :

                  t(4;14) Analysis:
                  100% of cells revealed 2 orange signals of FGF3 of locus 4p16.3 and 2 green
                  signals of IGH of locus 14q32.

                  t(11;14) Analysis:
                  63% of cells revealed 3 orange signals of MYEOV of locus 11q13 and 2 green
                  signals of IGH of locus 14q32.

                  IgH Translocation Analysis:
                  Results: Signal Pattern
                  100% of interphase revealed 2 normal copies of orange/green signal of IgH of
                  locus 14q32 .
                  100% of metaphase cells revealed intact orange/green signal of IGH at locus q32 of
                  both the homologues of 14.

                              Dr. PRATIBHA AMARE
                                  Cytogeneticist

10.1.7.61 09/05/2008 10:39:47   Page 1 of 2

CANCER CYTOGENETICS
LABORATORY

TATA MEMORIAL HOSPITAL

Dr. Ernest Borges Marg, Parel, Mumbai-400 012. India.
Tel.: 24177000, Extn:4369, Fax: 022-24146937
E-mail: cancercytogeneticstmh@vsnl.com

CANCER CYTOGENETICS LABORATORY

Case No. RG/13342   Requisition No. VZZ/F1/08/001315   Lab No. CG1164/CD

Name   Mr. C K SREEDHARAN   Phone No 0

Sex / Age   M 60   Category/Status F/ Out Patient   Fax   0
Clinico-Hematological Diagnosis   Specimen Status OK

MOLECULAR CYTOGENETICS (FISH) REPORT   09/05/2008

INTERPRETATION   There was no evidence of t(11;14) or t(4;14) associated with Multiple Myeloma . There
was no evidence of IGH involved translocations associated with B- lymphoid malignancies.
Trisomy 11 was detected in (Freq 63%).

Dr. PRATIBHA AMARE
Cytogeneticist

19.1.7.61 09/05/2008 10:39:47

Page 2 of 2

CANCER CYTOGENETICS
LABORATORY

TATA MEMORIAL HOSPITAL

Dr. Ernest Borges Marg, Parel, Mumbai-400 012. India.
Tel.: 24177000, Extn:4369, Fax: 022-24146937
E-mail: cancercytogeneticstmh@vsnl.com

CANCER CYTOGENETICS LABORATORY

Case No. **RG/13342**	Requisition No. **VZZ/F1/08/001316**	Lab No. **CG1165/CD**
Name Mr. C K SREEDHARAN		Phone No 0
Sex / Age M 50	Category/Status F/ Out Patient	Fax 0
Referred By HINDUJA HOSP		Req. Dt 24/04/2008
Clinical Details At Diagnosis		Specimen Type Bone Marrow Aspiration
Clinico-Hematological Diagnosis		Specimen Status OK

MOLECULAR CYTOGENETICS (FISH) REPORT   09/05/2008

Method	:	Direct Harvesting of Bone Marrow Aspirate/Peripheral Blood, Lymph Node Fluorescence in situ hybridization on interphase and metaphase cells
Test	:	Analysis of deletions of 13q and p53.
Probes/Probe panel	:	Vysis Inc locus specific (13q14) probe and Vysis Inc. locus specific p53 probe
Number of Cells Analyzed	:	200
Result	:	P53 deletion Analysis: 99% of interphase cells revealed 2 orange signals of p53 of locus17p13 100% of metaphase cells revealed intact orange signal of p53 at locus p13 of both the homologues of 17.
		Del(13q) Analysis: 98% of cells revealed 2 orange signal of locus 13q14.3.
INTERPRETATION		There was no evidence of p53 deletion or 13q deletion.

Dr. PRATIBHA AMARE
Cytogeneticist

10.1.7.61 09/05/2008 10.42.11

Page 1 of 1

CANCER CYTOGENETICS LABORATORY

The Treatment

'Everyday you are alive is an important day for you and those who love you. Yes, overcoming cancer is a journey, one that you didn't ask for. Some days will be exhausting...surgery, chemo and even radiation. But remember, everyday you open your eyes is a good day; the next will be better.'
- Becca Foundation

On 23/04/2008 Dr. Sachin Almel called me and my wife to his chamber and explained the complete course of treatment I had to undergo in the coming days to treat my disease. The doctor explained that there was a well established treatment procedure for multiple myeloma all over the world and the same treatment would be given to me at Hinduja Hospital.

This meant that the treatment procedure followed by the hospital was at par with the treatment procedure followed in the best hospitals around the world. As we had already seen and experienced the quality of medical facility and the expertise of the panel of doctors at Hinduja Hospital, we were convinced and had little doubt about the capability of the doctors at Hinduja Hospital.

Dr. Sachin Almel said that the line of treatment for me would be:

- Several cycles of chemotherapy, usually ranging from 4 to 6 cycles, depending on the response and the progress shown by me;
- Along with the chemotherapy other suitable steroids would also be administered;
- The chemotherapy would be continued till bone morrow was in remission.
- Once bone morrow was in remission and the patient shows substantial progress, a complete re-examination of various parameters of the patient would be carried out to ensure the condition of the patient to undertake stem cell transplant successfully;
- If the patient's health condition was satisfactory, stem cells would be mobilized from the patient's body in case of 'Autologous Stem Cell Transplant';

- Administration of heavy single dose of chemotherapy to completely destroy the existing blood cells;
- Stem Cell transplant; and
- Monitoring the response of the patient to transplant especially, platelet and haemoglobin levels.

Chemotherapy

Chemotherapy generally follows a certain pre-determined cycles with a specific frequency. Each cycle of chemotherapy will comprise several doses of chemotherapy drug, which would be administered intravenously.

In my case each chemotherapy cycle comprised of administration of 2 mg of chemo drug per session on four different days with the following frequency:

First Cycle of chemotherapy was administered on first day, fourth day, seventh day and on eleventh day. Second cycle of chemotherapy would again start from 21 st. day counted from first dose of the previous cycle. The remaining cycles would follow the same frequency.

Frequency of chemotherapy followed in my case is given in table 1.

Table 1- Chemotherapy and steroids frequency

Cycle	Drug / date	Drug / date	Drug / date	Drug / date
First	24/04/2008 B / Z / D	27/04/2008 B	30/04/2008 B	05/05/2008 B
Second	16/05/2008 B / Z / D	19/05/2008 B	22/05/2008 B	26/05/2008 B
Third	06/06/2008 B / Z / D	09/06/2008 B	12/06/2008 B	16/06/2008 B
Fourth	02/07/2008 B / Z / D	05/07/2008 B	08/07/2008 B	11/07/2008 B

(In the above table, 'B' indicates Bortenate, 'Z' indicates Zoldonat and 'D' indicates Dexona.)

Bortenate 2 mg was used as a chemotherapy drug and it was administered intravenously. Along with Bortenate, steroids –

Zoldonat and Dexona were administered. Thalidomide tablet was also prescribed and was taken orally. Zoldonat is used to treat hypercalcaemia of malignancy. Dexona (Dexamethasone) is used with chemotherapy to relieve some cancer medication's side effects such as nausea, vomiting, and loss of appetite.

Both Zoldonat and Dexona were administered intravenously.

Details of my chemotherapy and steroids treatments are given in the table 1.

Before every chemotherapy session, my complete blood (CBC) count was checked to ascertain the condition of the patient to undertake chemotherapy. Fortunately my CBC was normal before every chemo session, and all my chemotherapy cycles were completed as per protocol.

I want to highlight one more admirable aspect of Hinduja Hospital. Apart from the doctors, the entire nursing and the supporting staff were friendly, caring and professional in their conduct and behaviour. The nursing staff was competent, efficient and patient friendly. They were in rotation and as my course of treatment went on for several months, I had the opportunity to meet most of them. I shared an excellent rapport with them. Since they knew that I had to travel a long distance, they ensured my chemo session was taken up on priority, whenever possible. This was a memorable experience which I would remember forever.

By the time I completed my third cycle of chemo, I became increasingly restless and anxious to complete the remaining chemotherapy sessions. I felt weak and drained out. The sessions became monotonous. Added to these miseries, for each chemotherapy session I had to travel about 110 kilometers by road to come to the hospital (Kalyan to Mahim and back). I could not utilize the services of the local suburban train networks which were less expensive and fast since they were extremely crowded. Also I had to avoid public transport services due to the possibility of catching up infection. Each time I hired a private taxi to come to the hospital, which was not only time consuming but also quite expensive. This expensive travel further drained out my limited resources.

Till the completion of the second cycle of chemotherapy session I travelled alone. During third and fourth cycles of chemotherapy, either my wife or my brother in law accompanied me to the hospital as I had become weak and lost confidence.

Cancer is no doubt a life threatening disease. But more than the disease, it is the cost of treatment and the mental turmoil, the patient undergoes, really kill the patient. Cancer treatment is very expensive in India, since most of the drugs are patented by the multinational corporations and are mainly imported. A reasonably well to do person, say for example, a person of my status, may just be able to manage to meet the cost of treatment by borrowing from close relatives, by liquidating all possible savings and tangible assets. A poor and underprivileged patient can't even dream of managing the cost of treatment all by oneself.

In most cases, the actual expenses incurred, invariably overshoot the initial estimate by a wide margin. This usually happens due to the fact that, during the treatment, the doctor may consider it necessary to use some extra course of treatment due to the unexpected emerging situations. This further adds to the cost of overall treatment.

In the beginning of my treatment itself I had brought to the notice of Dr. Sachin Almel, about my financial constraint. Dr. Sachin assured me that he would help me in all possible ways to cut down the cost of treatment. Dr. Sachin Almel requested the stockists of Bortenate, the expensive chemotherapy drug, and the growth factor drug Neupogen to supply to me at the dealer's price, which was almost 15 to 20% less than the retail price. This helped me to save substantially as many doses of these drugs were administered during the course of my treatment. Dr. Sachin Almel also helped me with an appeal letter, which I used to raise donations from individuals and charity organizations. I could raise substantial contributions through this appeal letter. I can never forget the kind of help and moral support extended by Dr. Sachin Almel. My entire family is indebted to him for his kind humanitarian gesture and support.

My fourth cycle of chemotherapy was completed on 11/07/2008.

Dr. Sachin Almel told me that I had made satisfactory progress and I would not require any further course of chemotherapy, if I decided to undergo stem cell transplant. I was extremely happy for getting relieved from the chemotherapy sessions and agreed for stem cell transplant.

Dr. Sachin Almel informed me that the protocol demanded a complete examination of various body parameters of the patient who had undergone several sessions of chemotherapy to reconfirm the condition before stem cell transplant. As per the protocol following tests were conducted:

1. Complete Blood Count;
2. Freelite chains;
3. Antimicrobial susceptibility test;
4. General Body Profile;
5. Spirometry;
6. X-Ray of chest PA;
7. Colour Doppler Echo Test;
8. MRI of the whole body; and
9. Creatinine clearance test.

The above tests were conducted on 07/08/2008 and on 09/08/2008. Scanned copies of reports of the above examinations are attached. The reports were normal and Dr. Sachin Almel advised me to get admitted for stem cell mobilization during the second week of September.

I consulted Dr. Sachin Almel again on 03/09/2008 for stem cell mobilization. He advised me to get admitted on 13/09/2008 for stem cell mobilization. He also advised me to take the injection of Neupogen drug every day commencing from 05/09/2008 from my family physician. Neupogen is a white blood growth factor, which promotes production of stem cells.

My family doctor Dr. Vivek Bhosale administered Neupogen daily as advised.

P. D. HINDUJA NATIONAL HOSPITAL
& MEDICAL RESEARCH CENTRE
(Established and managed by the National Health & Education Society)

VEER SAVARKAR MARG, MAHIM, MUMBAI - 400 016, INDIA
PHONE : 2445 1515, 2445 2222, 2444 9199 FAX : 2444 9151

Date: 5th May, 2008

TO WHOM IT MAY CONCERN

Mr. C K Sreedharan, HH No. 1000298 is suffering from Multiple Myeloma.

Patient will need Chemotherapy for 6 Cylces

Each cycle costs approximately Rs. 75,000 to 1 lakh.

Total cost approximately Rs. 6 Lakhs.

Patient needs monetary support. Your help will take him long way.

The cheque can be drawn in favour of "P.D. Hinduja National Hospital & Medical Research Centre" with your covering letter.

If any queries, please do not hesitate to contact us.

Dr. Sachin Almel

Medical Oncology Consultant

24447006/9820229481

DR. SACHIN V. ALMEL
MD., DM., (Med. Onco)
CONSULTANT ONCOLOGIST,
Reg. No. G6527

P. D. HINDUJA NATIONAL HOSPITAL
& MEDICAL RESEARCH CENTRE
(Established and managed by the National Health & Education Society)

VEER SAVARKAR MARG, MAHIM, MUMBAI - 400 016, INDIA
PHONE : 2445 1515, 2445 2222, 2444 9199 FAX : 2444 9151

Date: 5th May, 2008

To Whom It May Concern

Mr C K Sreedharan, HH No.1000298 is suffering from Multiple Myeloma. The Department of Oncology is treating him for the same at P.D. Hinduja National Hospital & Medical Research Centre, Mumbai. He will require   chemotherapy

He has been assessed by the hospital social worker. He needs further financial assistance to enable him to continue treatment. We seek your assistance in this regard.

The cheque can be drawn in favour of P.D. Hinduja National Hospital & Medical Research Centre with your covering letter.

We thank you for your philanthropy and help.

Sincerely,

Avani Bhatia
Counselor/co-ordinator.
oncology dept.
Cell no.9967594148

P. D. HINDUJA NATIONAL HOSPITAL
& MEDICAL RESEARCH CENTRE

VEER SAVARKAR MARG, MAHIM, MUMBAI - 400 016, INDIA
PHONE : 2445 1515, 2445 2222, 2444 9199   FAX : 2444 9151

Date: 1st Aug, 2008

TO WHOM IT MAY CONCERN

Mr C K Sreedharan, HH No1000298, is suffering from Multiple Myeloma.

Patient will need Bone marrow Transplant. Approximate cost of the same is 4

to 5 lakhs.

Patient needs monetary support. Your help will take him long way.

The cheque can be drawn in favour of "P.D. Hinduja National Hospital &

Medical Research Centre" with your covering letter.

If any queries, please do not hesitate to contact us.

Dr. Sachin Almel
Medical Oncology Consultant
24447006/9820229481

DR. SACHIN V. ALMEL
MD, DM, (Med. Onco)
CONSULTANT ONCOLOGIST,
Reg. No. G5527

80

P. D. HINDUJA NATIONAL HOSPITAL
& MEDICAL RESEARCH CENTRE
(Established and managed by the National Health & Education Society)

VEER SAVARKAR MARG, MAHIM, MUMBAI - 400 016. INDIA
PHONE : 2445 1515, 2445 2222, 2444 9199 FAX : 2444 9161

DEPARTMENT OF LABORATORY MEDICINE
HEMATOLOGY

ORDER NO.   :   11431152   HH NO. :   1000298   ADM. NO. :

NAME   : C K SREEDHARAN   AGE   50 YEARS   SEX   : MALE

DATE   : 07/08/2008   LOCATION   : OPD   REFERRED BY DR.   : ALMEL SACHIN V

Samp. Coll Dt : 07/08/2008 01:19:27PM   WorkSht.DtTm: 07/08/2008 01:33:23PM

COMPLETE BLOOD COUNT

Test	Result	Units	Abnormality	Reference Range	
RED CELL COUNT	5.20	10^12/l		4.50 -	6.50
HEMOGLOBIN	13.90	g/dl		13.00 -	18.00
HEMATOCRIT	42.50	%		40.00 -	54.00
MCV	81.70	fl		76.00 -	96.00
MCH	26.70	pg	L	27.00 -	32.00
MCHC	32.70	g/dl		30.00 -	35.00
RDW	16.00	%	H	11.50 -	14.50
PLATELET COUNT	376.00	10^9/l		150.00 -	400.00
MPV	10.00	fl		6.80 -	12.60
WBC & DIFF COUNT					
WBC Count	9.45	10^9/l		4.00 -	11.00
Diff. WBC Count					
Neutrophils	67.00	%		40.00 -	75.00
Eosinophils	0.00	%	L	1.00 -	6.00
Lymphocytes	23.00	%		20.00 -	45.00
Monocytes	10.00	%		2.00 -	10.00
Basophils	0.00	%		0.00 -	1.00

* * End of Report * *

DR. S.KHODAIJI / DR. S GHOSH / DR. A. S. DESHPANDE
Consultant, Hematologist
Report Printed On   07-Aug-2008 16:56

P. D. HINDUJA NATIONAL HOSPITAL
& MEDICAL RESEARCH CENTRE
(Established and managed by the National Health & Education Society)

VEER SAVARKAR MARG, MAHIM, MUMBAI - 400 016, INDIA
PHONE : 2445 1515, 2445 2222, 2444 9199 FAX : 2444 9151

DEPARTMENT OF LABORATORY MEDICINE
BIOCHEMISTRY

ORDER NO.   :   11431152   HH NO. : 1000298   ADM. NO :

NAME   : C K SREEDHARAN   AGE   · 50 YEARS   SEX   : MALE

DATE   : 07/08/2008   LOCATION : OPD   REFERRED BY DR.   : ALMEL SACHIN V

Samp. Coll Dt   07/08/2008 01:22:42PM   WorkSht.DtTm   07/08/2008 01:33:23PM

Stat Lab

FREELITE CHAINS

Test	Result	Units	Status	Reference Range
FREE KAPPA LIGHT CHAIN	< 3.00 *	mg/L	L	3.30 - 19.40
FREE LAMBDA LIGHT CHAIN	< 4.00 *	mg/L	L	5.71 - 26.30

Comments : ✳ i.e. lowest measurable level.

* * End of Report * *

DR. T. F. ASHAVAID

Consultant Biochemist
Report Printed On :   07-Aug-2008 17:23

P. D. HINDUJA NATIONAL HOSPITAL
& MEDICAL RESEARCH CENTRE
(Established and managed by the National Health & Education Society)

VEER SAVARKAR MARG, MAHIM, MUMBAI 400 016, INDIA
PHONE : 2445 1515, 2445 2222, 2444 9199 FAX : 2444 9151

DEPARTMENT OF LABORATORY MEDICINE
BIOCHEMISTRY

ORDER NO.   : 11431152   HH NO. : 1000298   ADM. NO.   :

NAME   : C K SREEDHARAN   AGE   : 50 YEARS   SEX   : MALE

DATE   : 07/08/2008   LOCATION   : OPD   REFERRED BY DR.   : ALMEL SACHIN V

Samp Coll Dt   07/08/2008 01:19.27PM   WorkSht.DtTm   07/08/2008 01:33:23PM

Main Lab

GENERAL BODY PROFILE

Test		Result	Units	Status	Reference Range
Random Blood Glucose	Conventional	103.00	mg/dl		
	S.I.	5.67	mmol/l		
Random Urine Glucose		SNR			
Sodium	Conventional	134.80	mEq /l	L	135.00 - 147.0
	S.I.	134.80	mmol/l		135.00 - 147.00
Potassium	Conventional	4.90	mEq/l	H	3.30 - 4.80
	S.I.	4.90	mmol/l		3.30 - 4.80
Chloride	Conventional	106.10	mEq/l		101.00 - 111.0
	S.I.	106.10	mmol/l		101.00 - 111.00
TCO2	Conventional	23.80	mmol/l		23.00 - 27.00
	S.I.	23.80	mmol/l		23.00 - 27.00
Anion Gap	Conventional	9.80	mEq/l		8.00 - 12.00
	S.I.	9.80	mmol/l		8.00 - 12.00
Blood Urea Nitrogen	Conventional	8.00	mg/dl		5.00 - 25.00
	S.I.	2.86	mmol/l		1.79 - 8.93
Osmolality (calculated)		268.30	mOsm/l	L	280.00 - 295.00

DR. T. F. ASHAVAID

Consultant Biochemist
Report Printed On :   07-Aug-2008 16:41

P. D. HINDUJA NATIONAL HOSPITAL
& MEDICAL RESEARCH CENTRE
(Established and managed by the National Health & Education Society)

VEER SAVARKAR MARG, MAHIM, MUMBAI - 400 016, INDIA
PHONE : 2445 1515, 2445 2222, 2444 9199 FAX : 2444 9151

DEPARTMENT OF LABORATORY MEDICINE
BIOCHEMISTRY

ORDER NO. : 11431152   HH NO. : 1000298   ADM. NO. :

NAME : C K SREEDHARAN   AGE : 50 YEARS   SEX : MALE

DATE : 07/08/2008   LOCATION : OPD   REFERRED BY DR. : ALMEL SACHIN V

Samp. Coll Dt   07/08/2008 01:19:27PM   WorkSht.DtTm   07/08/2008 01:33:23PM

Main Lab

GENERAL BODY PROFILE

Test		Result	Units	Status	Reference Range	
Creatinine	Conventional	0.70	mg/dl		0.70 -	1.31
	S.I.	61.88	umol/l		61.88 -	115.80
Calcium	Conventional	9.30	mg/dl		8.00 -	10.40
	S.I.	2.33	mmol/l		2.00 -	2.60
Total Protein	Conventional	7.20	g/dl		6.70 -	8.20
	S.I.	72.00	g/l		67.00 -	82.00
Albumin	Conventional	4.60	g/dl		3.50 -	5.00
	S.I.	46.00	g/l		35.00 -	50.00
Globulin	Conventional	2.60	g/dl		2.60 -	4.10
	S.I.	26.00	g/l		26.00 -	41.00
A/G Ratio		1.80			1.20 -	2.50
Bilirubin(Total)	Conventional	0.70	mg/dl		0.20 -	1.00
	S.I.	11.97	umol/l		3.42 -	17.10
SGOT	Conventional	12.00	U/l	L	15.00 -	48.00
	S.I.	12.00	IU/l		15.00 -	48.00
SGPT	Conventional	14.00	U/l		10.00 -	40.00
	S.I.	14.00	IU/l		10.00 -	40.00

DR. T. F. ASHAVAID

Consultant Biochemist
Report Printed On :   07-Aug-2008 16:41

P. D. HINDUJA NATIONAL HOSPITAL
& MEDICAL RESEARCH CENTRE
(Established and managed by the National Health & Education Society)

VEER SAVARKAR MARG, MAHIM, MUMBAI - 400 016, INDIA
PHONE : 2445 1515, 2445 2222, 2444 9199 FAX : 2444 9151

DEPARTMENT OF LABORATORY MEDICINE
BIOCHEMISTRY

ORDER NO. : 11431152	HH NO. : 1000298	ADM. NO. :	
NAME : C K SREEDHARAN	AGE : 50 YEARS	SEX : MALE	
DATE : 07/08/2008 LOCATION : OPD	REFERRED BY DR. : ALMEL SACHIN V		
Samp. Coll Dt 07/08/2008 01:18:27PM	WorkSht.DtTm 07/08/2008 01:33:23PM		

Main Lab

GENERAL BODY PROFILE

Test	Result		Units	Status	Reference Range	
Alkaline Phosphatase	Conventional	71.00	U/l		40.00 -	120.0
	S.I.	71.00	IU/l		40.00 -	120.00
Gamma G.T.	Conventional	21.00	U/l		0.00 -	60.00
	S.I.	21.00	IU/l		0.00 -	60.00
Method :						

Comments : RBS AT 1:20 pm.

* * End of Report * *

DR. T. F. ASHAVAID

Consultant Biochemist

Report Printed On : 07-Aug-2008 16:41

Test Date :9.8.2008

P.D.HINDUJA NATIONAL HOSPITAL
and Medical Research Centre
Veer Savarkar Marg,Mahim,Mumbai-400 016

Last Name:	C.K.	First Name:	SREEDHARAN
Identification:	11440396	Age:	50 Years
Sex:	male	Height:	158 cm
Weight:	54 kg	Smoker:	N.S.
Ward:	OPD	Pred. Module:	INDIAN
Operator:	--	Physician:	DR S.ALMEL

SPIROMETRY

		Pred	Pre	% Pred
FVC	[L]	2.80	2.95	105.2
FEV 1	[L]	2.40	2.48	103.5
FEV 1 % FVC	[%]	79.33	84.15	106.1
FEF 25/75	[L/s]	2.31	2.89	125.0
FEF 25	[L/s]	5.24	10.54	200.9
FEF 50	[L/s]	2.99	4.01	134.1
FEF 75	[L/s]	1.11	0.95	85.4
PEF	[L/s]	6.29	11.55	183.7
FIF 50	[L/s]		7.08	
FIV1	[L]		2.88	
PIF	[L/s]		7.58	
MVV	[L/min]	86.87	157.5	181.3

C.K. SREEDHARAN HINDUJA HCHKUP   2

86

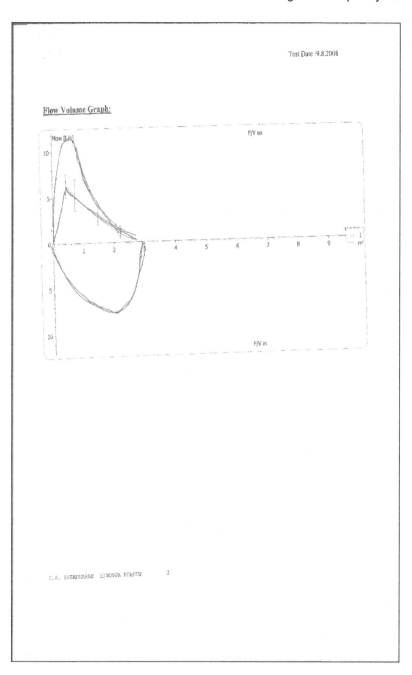

Flow Volume Graph:

P. D. HINDUJA NATIONAL HOSPITAL
& MEDICAL RESEARCH CENTRE
(Established and managed by the National Health & Education Society)

VEER SAVARKAR MARG, MAHIM, MUMBAI - 400 016, INDIA
PHONE : 2445 1515, 2445 2222, 2444 9199 FAX : 2444 9151

DEPARTMENT OF PULMONARY FUNCTION LAB

NAME	: C K SREEDHARAN	AGE : 50 YEARS	SEX : MALE
HH NO.	: 1000298	LOCATION : Out-Patient	ADM NO: –
REFERRED BY : DR. ALMEL SACHIN V		ORDER NO.: 11440396	DATE : 09/08/2008

Spirometry and flow volume loop within normal limits.

DR. Z.F. UDWADIA
MD,DNB, FRCP(London), FCCP(USA)
CONSULTANT CHEST PHYSICIAN

Report printed on : 09/08/2008 12:04 PM   Page 1 of 1

88

P. D. HINDUJA NATIONAL HOSPITAL
& MEDICAL RESEARCH CENTRE
(Established and managed by the National Health & Education Society)

VEER SAVARKAR MARG, MAHIM, MUMBAI - 400 016, INDIA
PHONE : 2445 1515, 2445 2222, 2444 9199 FAX : 2444 9151

DEPARTMENT OF IMAGING

NAME	: C K SREEDHARAN		AGE : 50 YEARS	SEX	: MALE
HH NO.	: 1000298	LOCATION : OPD	ADM NO : -	EXAM NO.	: 13519
REFERRED BY	: DR. ALMEL SACHIN V		ORDER NO. : 11440396	DATE	: 09/08/2008

EXAMINATION
X-RAY CHEST PA

REPORT DETAILS

High KV frontal chest radiograph shows normal soft tissues and bony cage.

The cardiac size is within normal limits and the cardiac silhoutte is normal.

Both lung fields are clear. The pleural spaces are clear. No hilar, diaphragmatic or mediastinal lesion is seen.

CONCLUSION :- NORMAL X - RAY OF CHEST.

DR. J.M. MODHE - M.D.
CONSULTANT - RADIOLOGIST

sr/9.8.08

Report printed on : 09/08/2008 01:32 PM   Page 1 of 1

P. D. HINDUJA NATIONAL HOSPITAL
& MEDICAL RESEARCH CENTRE
(Established and managed by the National Health & Education Society)

VEER SAVARKAR MARG, MAHIM, MUMBAI - 400 016, INDIA
PHONE : 2445 1515, 2445 2222, 2444 9199 FAX : 2444 9151

DEPARTMENT OF NON - INVASIVE CARDIOLOGY

NAME:	: C K SREEDHARAN	AGE : 50 YEARS	SEX : MALE
HH NO.	: 1000298	LOCATION : Out-Patient	ADM NO: -
REFERRED BY : DR. ALMEL SACHIN V		ORDER NO.: 11440396	DATE : 09/08/2008

ECHO WITH COLOR DOPPLER
Background : For bone marrow transplantation, multiple myeloma. Post chemotherapy.

* Cardiac chamber dimensions : Normal

* Septae : Intact

* Structure of cardiac valves : Normal

* Wall motion abnormalities : Apical anterior septum, apical inferior septum are mildly hypokinetic with preserved thickness

* LVEF : 50%, normal RVEF

* LV clot / vegetations : No

* Pericardial effusion : No

* IVC : Normal

Doppler Data:
* Mitral Inflow : E < A, E at A = 26 cm/sec
* DT = 222 msec   FPV : 46 cm/sec   IVRT : 94 msec
* MPAP = 34 mm of Hg by PAT
* Flow across all cardiac valves : Normal
* Pulmonary venous flow : Normal
* PVA duration = 100 msec, MVA duration = 72 msec
* MPI (LV) = 0.39

CONCLUSION:
* Normal LV size
* RWMA as above
* LVEF 50%
* Grade I diastolic dysfunction
* No PAH

DR.ACHYUT
CLINICAL ASSISTANT

DR. C.K.PONDE
CONSULTANT CARDIOLOGIST

Report printed on 09/08/2008 05:22 PM

Page 1 of 2

P. D. HINDUJA NATIONAL HOSPITAL
& MEDICAL RESEARCH CENTRE
(Established and managed by the National Health & Education Society)

VEER SAVARKAR MARG, MAHIM, MUMBAI - 400 016, INDIA
PHONE : 2445 1515, 2445 2222, 2444 9199 FAX : 2444 9151

DEPARTMENT OF LABORATORY MEDICINE

BLOOD BANK

ORDER NO. : 11431152   HH NO. : 1000298   ADM. NO. :

NAME : C K SREEDHARAN   AGE : 50 YEARS   SEX : MALE

DATE : 07/08/2008   LOCATION : : OPD   REFERRED BY : DR. ALMEL SACHIN V

Test	Results
HIV ANTIGEN & ANTIBODY (I &II) (MEIA)	NEGATIVE
HEPATITIS B (HBsAg) (MEIA)	NEGATIVE
HCV ANTIBODY (MEIA)	NEGATIVE

MEIA - Microparticle Enzyme Immunoassay

DR.A.S.DESHPANDE / DR. S. KHODAIJI

Consultant Transfusion Medicine & Hematology

Report Printed On : 07-Aug-2008 15:36

P. D. HINDUJA NATIONAL HOSPITAL
& MEDICAL RESEARCH CENTRE
(Established and managed by the National Health & Education Society)

VEER SAVARKAR MARG, MAHIM, MUMBAI - 400 016, INDIA
PHONE : 2445 1515, 2445 2222, 2444 9199 FAX : 2444 9151

DEPARTMENT OF IMAGING

NAME	: C K SREEDHARAN	AGE	: 50 YEARS	SEX : MALE
HH NO.	: 1000298 LOCATION : OPD	ADM NO.	: -	EXAM NO. : MRI 29122
REFERRED BY	: DR. ALMEL SACHIN V	ORDER NO. : 11443264	DATE	: 09/06/2008

EXAMINATION
MRI OF THE WHOLE BODY SCREENING.
REPORT DETAILS

Multiplanar multiecho MR of whole body screening has been performed.

Patient is a known case of multiple myeloma on chemotherapy.

Diffuse mottling of the marrow of all the vertebrae as well as the pelvic bones is visualised on T1 weighted images. Some of the lesions display focal hyperintensity on the T2 weighted images. Wedging of an upper dorsal vertebra is seen.

Visualised bones of the upper and lower limbs display normal fatty marrow.

CONCLUSION: Diffuse T1 mottling is noted within the marrow of the vertebrae as well as the pelvic bones consistent with known multiple myeloma. Wedge compression fracture of an upper dorsal vertebra is noted.

DR. SMRUTI MULANI MD,DNB
Consultant Radiologist
lf
11-08-08

P. D. HINDUJA NATIONAL HOSPITAL
& MEDICAL RESEARCH CENTRE
(Established and managed by the National Health & Education Society)

VEER, SAVARKAR MARG, MAHIM, MUMBAI - 400 016, INDIA
PHONE : 2445 1515, 2445 2222, 2444 9199 FAX : 2444 9151

DEPARTMENT OF LABORATORY MEDICINE
BIOCHEMISTRY

ORDER NO. : 11440256	HH NO : 1000298	ADM. NO. :	
NAME : C K SREEDHARAN	AGE : 50 YEARS	SEX : MALE	
DATE : 09/08/2008 LOCATION : OPD	REFERRED BY DR. : ALMEL SACHIN V		
Samp. Coll Dt 09/08/2008 09:54:11AM	WorkSht.DtTm 09/08/2008 10:08:35AM		

Main Lab

CREATININE CLEARANCE TEST

Test		Result	Units	Status	Reference Range
Urine Volume		2,600.00	ml/24hrs		
Serum Creatinine	Conventional	0.70	mg/dl		0.60 - 1.10
	S.I.	61.88	umol/l		53.04 - 97.34
Urinary Creatinine	Conventional	1,066.00	mg/24hrs		800.00 - 2000.0
	S.I.	93.81	mmol/24hrs		70.40 - 176.00
Body Surface Area		1.53	m.sq		
24 hrs Creatinine Clearance		119.58	ml/min	H	80.00 - 110.00

* * End of Report * *

DR. T. F. ASHAVAID

Consultant Biochemist
Report Printed On : 09-Aug-2008 13:47

Stem cell mobilization
General information

Stem cells are early, immature cells that are produced in the bone marrow. They can grow into any type of blood cell- a white cell to fight infection, a red cell to carry oxygen or a platelet to help clot the blood.

There are two types of stem cell transplants- autologous and allogeneic.

In autologous stem cell transplantation, the stem cells are removed from a person, stored, and later given back to that same person. In this case, the patient is the own donor.

Allogeneic stem cell transplantation involves transferring the stem cells from a healthy person (the donor) to the body of the patient.

There are two methods which are generally adopted for collecting enough stem cells for a transplant.

Originally the collection was done by putting the donor under a general anesthesia, and using a series of needles to extract bone marrow from large bones, usually the pelvis. This procedure is generally referred as 'Bone Marrow Harvest.' The word 'harvest' refers to the product collected from the donor.

The Second type of harvest is 'Peripheral Blood Stem Cell Harvest.' In this method, the donor is seated in a chair and an IV is inserted in each of the arm. Blood is drawn out of one arm, sent to an aphaeresis machine where the stem cells are separated and the remaining blood is sent back into the IV in the other arm. In some cases a central venous catheter may be inserted if the patient does not have veins capable of accepting IV needles.

Presently, Peripheral Blood Stem Cell Harvest procedure is mostly used due to its several advantages. Normally there are not many stem cells circulating in the blood. Hence steps are taken to encourage the body to push huge quantities of stem cells out of the bone marrow and into the blood stream where they can be collected.

This is usually done by giving the donor a white blood growth factor. The brand name of this drug is Neupogen. This drug encourages the stem cells to mature very quickly into Neutrophils (a type of white blood cell). Because the drug causes such a rapid increase in Neutrophils, bone marrow is forced to push the stem cells out of the marrow and into the blood to make room for all the new cells.

Timing is very critical for mobilizing stem cells from the donor. Once the stem cells have been forced into the blood, they have a tendency to mature into Neutrophils as quickly as possible. Whole key to the procedure is to collect them before they do that, and while they are still uncommitted cells.

Usually it takes around 7 days after chemotherapy / Neupogen when maximum number of stem cells will be circulating. Usually the donor from whom the stem cells are to be mobilized is given Neupogen every day, starting from seven to ten days before the planned stem cell mobilization. A simple blood test of the donor will be done to find the optimum day. The harvest procedure is generally painless and quite simple for the donor.

Platelets donation

The same aphaeresis machine and method is also used for platelet donations. The machine separates platelets and returns the remaining blood contents through the needle in the other arm.

As advised I got admitted on 13/09/2008 for stem cell mobilization. I was to undergo 'autologous stem cell transplant', which required stem cells to be mobilized from my blood. My CBC was monitored on a daily basis for deciding appropriate time for stem cell mobilization. I was given Neupogen injection daily. It was found that on 17/09/2008 and on 19/09/2008, my CBC was satisfactory for carrying out stem cell mobilization.

On 17/09/2008 and on 19/09/2008 stem cells were mobilized from my blood as per the procedure already explained.

Following scanned copies of the reports are attached:

1. The CBC report on 14/09/2009, the first day after admission;

2. The CBC report on 17/09/2008, the day the first phase of stem cell mobilization was done;

3. The CBC report on 19/09/2008, the day the second phase of stem cell mobilization was done; and

4. Discharge report.

I was discharged on 20/09/2008 and was advised to get admitted on 30/09/2008 for stem cell transplant. Dr. Sachin Almel also informed that I might need platelet transfusions after stem cell transplant and advised me to keep donors from friends and relatives circles ready, in case of the need.

The mobilized stem cells were stored in blood bank under controlled conditions. On 22/09/2008 the mobilized stem cells were tested. There was no growth observed and the mobilized stem cells were declared fit for transplantation.

Scanned copies of reports of department of microbiology are attached in the following pages.

Tata Memorial Hospital provides a low cost online second opinion service on cancer diagnosis. Patients can get a second opinion on their cancer diagnosis and treatment from one of the 90 doctors of the Tata Memorial Centre promoted National Cancer Grid without visiting the hospital.

Patients can email their reports, upload scans or seek advice on WhatsApp.

A call center (Navya) helps people with the reports to be uploaded. It prepares a medical report that is sent to doctors by email or WhatsApp.

The doctor usually needs only a few minutes to give the opinion, spelling out a diagnosis as well as a treatment plan.

The process takes 24 hours usually, but could stretch up to three days.

Tata Memorial Hospital's doctors give their opinion for free, but a fee of Rs. 6000 is charged for daily operations.

At present, 90 doctors from the Department of Atomic Energy-supported National Cancer Grid (NCG) are experts on the Navya panel. Around 100 hospitals that provide cancer treatment across the country are part of the grid.

(Source: Times of India, Mumbai edition dated 09 June, 2017)

P. D. HINDUJA NATIONAL HOSPITAL
& MEDICAL RESEARCH CENTRE
(Established and managed by the National Health & Education Society)

VEER SAVARKAR MARG, MAHIM, MUMBAI - 400 016, INDIA
PHONE : 2445 1515, 2445 2222, 2444 9199 FAX : 2444 9151

DEPARTMENT OF LABORATORY MEDICINE
BIOCHEMISTRY

ORDER NO. : 11605682

HH NO. : 1000298 ADM. NO. : 1085808

NAME : C K SREEDHARAN

AGE : 50 YEARS SEX : MALE

DATE : 14/09/2008 LOCATION : 21S1

REFERRED BY DR. : ALMEL SACHIN V

Samp. Coll Dt : 14/09/2008 12:22:34PM

WorkSht.D(Tm : 14/09/2008 12:35:38PM

Stat Lab

Test		Result	Units	Status	Reference Range	
Sodium	Conventional	137.20	mEq /l		135.00 -	147.0
	S.I.	137.20	mmol/l		135.00 -	147.00
Potassium	Conventional	4.00	mEq/l		3.30 -	4.80
	S.I.	4.00	mmol/l		3.30 -	4.80
Creatinine	Conventional	0.80	mg/dl		0.70 -	1.31
	S.I.	70.72	umol/l		61.88 -	115.80

* * End of Report * *

DR. P. E. ASHAVAID   14/9/08
Consultant Biochemist
Report Printed On :   14-Sep-2008 16:23

P. D. HINDUJA NATIONAL HOSPITAL
& MEDICAL RESEARCH CENTRE
(Established and managed by the National Health & Education Society)

VEER SAVARKAR MARG, MAHIM, MUMBAI - 400 016, INDIA
PHONE : 2445 1515, 2445 2222, 2444 9199 FAX : 2444 9151

DEPARTMENT OF LABORATORY MEDICINE
HEMATOLOGY

ORDER NO. : 11618082	HH NO. : 1000298	ADM. NO. : 1085808
NAME : C K SREEDHARAN	AGE : 50 YEARS	SEX : MALE
DATE : 17/09/2008 LOCATION : 21S1	REFERRED BY DR. : ALMEL SACHIN V	
Samp. Coll Dt : 17/09/2008 03:04:43AM	WorkSht.DtTm: 17/09/2008 03:20:37AM	

COMPLETE BLOOD COUNT

Test	Result	Units	Abnormality	Reference Range
RED CELL COUNT	4.60	10^12/l		4.50 - 6.50
HEMOGLOBIN	12.60	g/dl	L	13.00 - 18.00
HEMATOCRIT	37.80	%	L	40.00 - 54.00
MCV	82.20	fl		76.00 - 96.00
MCH	27.40	pg		27.00 - 32.00
MCHC	33.30	g/dl		30.00 - 35.00
RDW	15.40	%	H	11.50 - 14.50
PLATELET COUNT	209.00	10^9/l		150.00 - 400.00
MPV	10.20	fl		6.80 - 12.60
WBC & DIFF COUNT				
WBC Count	17.55	10^9/l	H	4.00 - 11.00
Diff. WBC Count				
Neutrophils	82.00	%	H	40.00 - 75.00
Eosinophils	2.00	%		1.00 - 6.00
Lymphocytes	12.00	%	L	20.00 - 45.00
Monocytes	3.00	%		2.00 - 10.00
Basophils	1.00	%		0.00 - 1.00

* * End of Report * *

DR. S.KHODAIJI / DR. S GHOSH / DR. A. S. DESHPANDE
Consultant, Hematologist
Report Printed On : 17-Sep-2008 10:32

P. D. HINDUJA NATIONAL HOSPITAL
& MEDICAL RESEARCH CENTRE
(Established and managed by the National Health & Education Society)

VEER SAVARKAR MARG, MAHIM, MUMBAI - 400 016, INDIA
PHONE : 2445 1515, 2445 2222, 2444 9199 FAX : 2444 9151

DEPARTMENT OF LABORATORY MEDICINE
HEMATOLOGY

ORDER NO. : 11628779

HH NO. : 1000296   ADM. NO. : 1085908

NAME : C K SREEDHARAN

AGE : 50 YEARS   SEX : MALE

DATE : 19/09/2008   LOCATION : 21S1   REFERRED BY DR. : ALMEL SACHIN V

Samp. Coll Dt : 19/09/2008 03:19:52AM   WorkSht.DtTm: 19/09/2008 05:52:57AM

COMPLETE BLOOD COUNT

Test	Result	Units	Abnormality	Reference Range
RED CELL COUNT	4.15	$10^{12}/l$	L	4.50 - 6.50
HEMOGLOBIN	11.50	g/dl	L	13.00 - 18.00
HEMATOCRIT	34.70	%	L	40.00 - 54.00
MCV	83.60	fl		76.00 - 96.00
MCH	27.70	pg		27.00 - 32.00
MCHC	33.10	g/dl		30.00 - 35.00
RDW	15.30	%	H	11.50 - 14.50
PLATELET COUNT	144.00	$10^9/l$	L	150.00 - 400.00
MPV	10.50	fl		6.80 - 12.60
WBC & DIFF COUNT				
WBC Count	25.97	$10^9/l$	H	4.00 - 11.00
Diff. WBC Count				
Neutrophils	85.00	%	H	40.00 - 75.00
Eosinophils	2.00	%		1.00 - 6.00
Lymphocytes	7.00	%	L	20.00 - 45.00
Monocytes	5.00	%		2.00 - 10.00
Basophils	0.00	%		0.00 - 1.00
Band Cells	1.00	%		

Comments : Platelets : Borderline reduced.

* * End of Report * *

DR. S.KHODAIJI / DR. S GHOSH / DR. A. S. DESHPANDE
Consultant, Hematologist
Report Printed On :   19-Sep-2008 12:15

P. D. HINDUJA NATIONAL HOSPITAL
& MEDICAL RESEARCH CENTRE
(Established and managed by the National Health & Education Society)

VEER SAVARKAR MARG, MAHIM, MUMBAI - 400 016, INDIA
PHONE : 2445 1515, 2445 2222, 2444 9199 FAX : 2444 9151

DEPARTMENT OF MICROBIOLOGY

SAMPLES RECEIVED FOR TESTING PURPOSE

PATIENT NAME – C. K SHREEDHARAN

DATE : 22/09/2008   HH NO - 1000298   LOCATION : C/O BLOOD BANK

SITES   **CULTURE REPORT**

1. STEM CELLS PBSC IV$_A$ NO GROWTH

DR. CAMILLA RODRIGUES

MD

Consultant Microbiologist

P. D. HINDUJA NATIONAL HOSPITAL
& MEDICAL RESEARCH CENTRE
(Established and managed by the National Health & Education Society)

VEER SAVARKAR MARG, MAHIM, MUMBAI - 400 016, INDIA
PHONE : 2445 1515, 2445 2222, 2444 9199 FAX : 2444 9151

DEPARTMENT OF MICROBIOLOGY

SAMPLES RECEIVED FOR TESTING PURPOSE

PATIENT NAME – C. K SHREEDHARAN

DATE : 22/09/2008   IIH NO - 1000298   LOCATION : C/O BLOOD BANK

SITES   **CULTURE REPORT**

1. STEM CELLS PBSC IV_B NO GROWTH

DR. CAMILLA RODRIGUES

MD

Consultant Microbiologist

P. D. HINDUJA NATIONAL HOSPITAL
& MEDICAL RESEARCH CENTRE
(Established and managed by the National Health & Education Society)

VEER SAVARKAR MARG, MAHIM, MUMBAI - 400 016, INDIA
PHONE : 2445 1515, 2445 2222, 2444 9199 FAX : 2444 9151

DISCHARGE SUMMARY / CARD

Name : C K SREEDHARAN   Age : 50 Y   Sex : M
HH No : 1000298   Admission No : 1085808
Admission Date : 13/09/2008   Discharge Date : 20 | 9 | 2008
Location : 21S1

FINAL DIAGNOSIS:
Multiple myeloma

CHIEF COMPLAINTS AND HISTORY:
50 year old gentleman known case of multiple myeloma, post 4 cycles of treatment with
Bortinate. Bone marrow is in remission. Now planed for Autologous stem cell transplant.
Presently admitted for stem cell mobilization
C/o tingling and numbness in both feet and hands.

PERTINENT PHYSICAL FINDINGS:
O/E – Clinically stable

INVESTIGATIVE DATA:
On 14.09.08 – Hb 13.5   WBC 15,980   Platelet 2.08.000
Creat 0.8   Sodium 137.2   Potassium 4

TREATMENT GIVEN:
Patient received Inj. Neupogen 300mcg s/c BD on 14.09.08 followed by underwent stem
cell mobilization on 17.09.2008 and 19.09.08.

Patient tolerated procedure well.
Patient was started on T. Gabaneuron 300mcg 1-1-1
in view of peripheral neuropathy.

DISCHARGE ADVICE:
T. Gabaneuron 300mcg 1-1-1
Duvanta 20mg 0-0-1
Ativan 1mg 0-0-1

To advised to come and get admitted on 30.09.2008 for stem cell transplant.

Dr. ALMEL SACHIN V
CONSULTANT – ONCOLOGIST

RE:MRD/YV/20.09.2008

PLEASE BRING THIS DISCHARGE SUMMARY/CARD FOR FURTHER REFERENCE
"IN CASE OF EMERGENCY PLEASE REACH CASUALTY IMMEDIATELY"

Stem cell transplant

As explained earlier, in an autologous transplant, a patient's own blood-forming stem cells are collected. The patient is then treated with high doses of chemotherapy, or a combination of chemotherapy and radiation. High-dose treatment kills cancer cells, but also eliminates blood-producing cells that are left in the bone marrow. Afterwards, the collected stem cells are transplanted back into the patient, allowing bone marrow to produce new blood cells.

Usual procedure followed for stem cell transplant is given below:

1. Administration of high dose of chemotherapy to kill all blood-producing cells left in the bone marrow; and

2. The transplant of previously harvested stem cells immediately after a day or two of high dose chemotherapy.

The harvested stem cells are transplanted into the patient's bloodstream in the same way as that of blood transfusion. Over the following days and weeks, transplanted stem cells migrate to marrow space in the bones, where they gradually begin to produce new blood cells. Between two to three weeks after the transplant, newly formed blood cells can be detected in the patient's bloodstream. As the time passes, a successful transplant graft will produce red blood cells, white blood cells, and platelets.

During the initial periods immediately after the transplantation, the patients are to be very careful and need a great deal of medical attention and support. The patients may require many transfusions of irradiated red blood cells and platelets as well as antibiotics to prevent and treat bacterial, viral and fungal infections, which are most likely to occur in the first three months after the transplantation.

The patient who has undergone the transplant may need to remain in the hospital for several weeks after the transplant. During this time, precautionary measures are taken to protect the patient from possible infection. The patient is usually admitted in an isolation care center. People, who enter the room need to wear a clean sterilized apron, wear protective gloves and masks and wash their hands with antiseptic soap. Fresh fruits, flowers, plants or cut flowers are prohibited in the patient's room, as these can carry disease causing bacteria. The patient is also prohibited from eating any raw and uncooked food.

As advised during my stem cell mobilization time, I got admitted into Hinduja Hospital on 30/09/2008 for the planned stem cell transplantation. I was admitted in an isolated special care center.

My CBC was monitored daily to select the appropriate day for administering the high dose of chemotherapy drug. On 05/10/2008 my CBC was found satisfactory, and a high dose of Melphelan, a chemotherapy drug was administered intravenously. This was done by one of the most experienced and senior nurse Ms. Anitha. On the following day, on 06/10/2008, the stem cell transplant was carried out. After the transplant my CBC drastically came down. I have attached the scanned copies of my CBC reports before and after the stem cell transplant to show the effect of the high dose chemotherapy.

Post stem cell transplantation, I developed high Creatinine but it settled down on its own within 24 hours. On 12/10/2008 I developed fever and it did not respond to antibiotics. Ambisome, a very expensive, imported antibiotic was given for four days to treat fever.

The chemotherapy also had its own adverse side effects. I completely lost hair from all parts of the body, including the head. I developed painful sour mouth. I completely lost my appetite and the very sight of food repulsed me. I could not eat solid food and I refused to eat. My wife somehow forced me to eat some solid food. Solid food was mashed into liquid form, so that I could just force it down my throat. This was the time I gave maximum trouble and anxiety to my wife.

Post stem cell transplant, I was instructed to maintain maximum hygiene. I was made to take bath twice a day- morning and in the evening. Prior to my entry into the bathroom, it was thoroughly cleaned and sanitized. No one else other than the nursing staff were permitted to approach me. My wife could come near only after wearing the sanitized apron.

Some important scanned copies of test reports of post stem cell transplant are attached in the following pages.

P. D. HINDUJA NATIONAL HOSPITAL
& MEDICAL RESEARCH CENTRE
(Established and managed by the National Health & Education Society)

VEER SAVARKAR MARG, MAHIM, MUMBAI - 400 016, INDIA
PHONE : 2445 1515, 2445 2222, 2444 9199 FAX : 2444 9151

DEPARTMENT OF LABORATORY MEDICINE
BIOCHEMISTRY

ORDER NO. : 11693874   HH NO. : 1000298   ADM. NO. : 1088889

NAME   : C K SREEDHARAN   AGE   : 50 YEARS   SEX   : MALE

DATE   : 03/10/2008   LOCATION : 16S9   REFERRED BY DR.   : ALMEL SACHIN V

Samp. Coll Dt   03/10/2008 02:55:20AM   WorkSht.DtTm   03/10/2008 03:32:22AM

Stat Lab

GENERAL BODY PROFILE

Test		Result	Units	Status	Reference Range
Fasting Blood Glucose	Conventional	95.00	mg/dl		70.00 - 115.00
	S.I	5.23	mmol/l		3.85 - 6.33
Sodium	Conventional	138.90	mEq/l		135.00 - 147.0
	S.I	138.90	mmol/l		135.00 - 147.00
Potassium	Conventional	4.30	mEq/l		3.30 - 4.80
	S.I.	4.30	mmol/l		3.30 - 4.80
Chloride	Conventional	104.50	mEq/l		101.00 - 111.0
	S.I.	104.50	mmol/l		101.00 - 111.00
TCO2	Conventional	27.70	mmol/l	H	23.00 - 27.00
	S.I	27.70	mmol/l		23.00 - 27.00
Anion Gap	Conventional	11.00	mEq/l		8.00 - 12.00
	S.I	11.00	mmol/l		8.00 - 12.00
Blood Urea Nitrogen	Conventional	8.00	mg/dl		5.00 - 25.00
	S.I.	2.86	mmol/l		1.79 - 8.93
Osmolality (calculated)		275.50	mOsm/l	L	280.00 - 295.00
Creatinine	Conventional	0.90	mg/dl		0.70 - 1.31
	S.I.	79.56	umol/l		61.88 - 115.80

DR. T. F. ASHAVAID

Consultant Biochemist

Report Printed On :   03-Oct-2008 09:04

P. D. HINDUJA NATIONAL HOSPITAL
& MEDICAL RESEARCH CENTRE
(Established and managed by the National Health & Education Society)

VEER SAVARKAR MARG, MAHIM, MUMBAI - 400 016, INDIA
PHONE : 2445 1515, 2445 2222, 2444 9199 FAX : 2444 9151

DEPARTMENT OF LABORATORY MEDICINE
BIOCHEMISTRY

ORDER NO. : 11693874   HH NO. : 1000298   ADM. NO : 1086869

NAME : C K SREEDHARAN   AGE : 50 YEARS   SEX : MALE

DATE : 03/10/2008   LOCATION : 19S9   REFERRED BY DR. : ALMEL SACHIN V

Samp. Coll Dt   03/10/2008 02:55.20AM   WorkSht.DtTm   03/10/2008 03:32:22AM

Stat Lab

GENERAL BODY PROFILE

Test		Result	Units	Status	Reference Range	
Calcium	Conventional	9.40	mg/dl		8.00 -	10.40
	S.I.	2.35	mmol/l		2.00 -	2.60
Total Protein	Conventional	6.60	g/dl	L	6.70 -	8.20
	S.I.	66.00	g/l		67.00 -	82.00
Albumin	Conventional	3.90	g/dl		3.50 -	5.00
	S.I.	39.00	g/l		35.00 -	50.00
Globulin	Conventional	2.70	g/dl		2.60 -	4.10
	S.I.	27.00	g/l		26.00 -	41.00
A/G Ratio		1.40			1.20 -	2.50
Bilirubin(Total)	Conventional	0.70	mg/dl		0.20 -	1.00
	S.I.	11.97	umol/l		3.42 -	17.10
SGOT	Conventional	10.00	U/l	L	15.00 -	48.00
	S.I.	10.00	IU/l		15.00 -	48.00
SGPT	Conventional	13.00	U/l		10.00 -	40.00
	S.I.	13.00	IU/l		10.00 -	40.00
Alkaline Phosphatase	Conventional	43.00	U/l		40.00 -	120.0
	S.I.	43.00	IU/l		40.00 -	120.00

DR. T. F. ASHAVAID

Consultant Biochemist
Record Printed On :   03-Oct-2008 09:04

P. D. HINDUJA NATIONAL HOSPITAL
& MEDICAL RESEARCH CENTRE
(Established and managed by the National Health & Education Society)

VEER SAVARKAR MARG, MAHIM, MUMBAI - 400 016, INDIA
PHONE : 2445 1515, 2445 2222, 2444 9199 FAX : 2444 9151

DEPARTMENT OF LABORATORY MEDICINE
BIOCHEMISTRY

ORDER NO. : 11693874   HH NO. : 1000298   ADM. NO : 1086889

NAME   : C K SREEDHARAN   AGE   : 50 YEARS   SEX   : MALE

DATE   : 03/10/2008   LOCATION : 16S9   REFERRED BY DR   : ALMEL SACHIN V

Samp. Coll Dt   03/10/2008 02:55:20AM   WorkSht.DtTm   03/10/2008 03:32:22AM

Stat Lab

GENERAL BODY PROFILE

Test		Result	Units	Status	Reference Range
Gamma G.T.	Conventional	15.00	U/I		0.00 - 60.00
	S.I.	15.00	IU/I		0.00 - 60.00

* * End of Report * *

DR. T. F. ASHAVAID

Consultant Biochemist
Report Printed On :   03-Oct-2008 09:04

108

P. D. HINDUJA NATIONAL HOSPITAL
& MEDICAL RESEARCH CENTRE
(Established and managed by the National Health & Education Society)

VEER SAVARKAR MARG, MAHIM, MUMBAI - 400 016, INDIA
PHONE : 2445 1515, 2445 2222, 2444 9199 FAX : 2444 9151

DEPARTMENT OF LABORATORY MEDICINE

BLOOD BANK

ORDER NO: H.H.NO: 1000298   REG NO: 1086889

NAME : C.K.SREEDHARAN   AGE : 50 YRS   SEX: M

REFERRED BY : DR.SACHIN ALMEL   LOC: 16SW-09   Date: 04/10/2008

SAMPLE	VIABILITY RESULT
PBSC IV A (Peripheral blood stem cells)	95 %
1 day prior to infusion	
PBSC IV B (Peripheral blood stem cells)	98 %
1 day prior to infusion	

Comments :

DR. A.S. DESHPANDE/DR.S.KHODAIJI
Consultant Transfusion Medicine & Hematology

109

P. D. HINDUJA NATIONAL HOSPITAL
& MEDICAL RESEARCH CENTRE
(Established and managed by the National Health & Education Society)

VEER SAVARKAR MARG, MAHIM, MUMBAI - 400 016, INDIA
PHONE : 2445 1515, 2445 2222, 2444 9199 FAX : 2444 9151

DEPARTMENT OF LABORATORY MEDICINE
BIOCHEMISTRY

ORDER NO. : 11705455   HH NO. : 1000296   ADM. NO. : 1086889

NAME   : C K SREEDHARAN   AGE   : 50 YEARS   SEX   : MALE

DATE   : 05/10/2008   LOCATION   : 16S9   REFERRED BY DR.   : ALMEL SACHIN V

Samp. Coll Dt   05/10/2008 06:24:08PM   WorkSht.DtTm   05/10/2008 06:32:39PM

Main Lab

Test	Result		Units	Status	Reference Range	
Creatinine	Conventional	0.70	mg/dl		0.70 -	1.31
	S.I.	61.88	umol/l		61.88 -	115.80

DR. T. F. ASHAVAID

Consultant Biochemist

Report Printed On   05-Oct-2008 19:09

P. D. HINDUJA NATIONAL HOSPITAL
& MEDICAL RESEARCH CENTRE
(Established and managed by the National Health & Education Society)

VEER SAVARKAR MARG, MAHIM, MUMBAI - 400 016, INDIA
PHONE : 2445 1515, 2445 2222, 2444 9199 FAX : 2444 9151

DEPARTMENT OF LABORATORY MEDICINE
BIOCHEMISTRY

ORDER NO. : 11705455   HH NO. : 1000298   ADM. NO. : 1086889

NAME : C K SREEDHARAN   AGE : 50 YEARS   SEX : MALE

DATE : 05/10/2008   LOCATION : 16S9   REFERRED BY DR : ALMEL SACHIN V

Samp. Coll Dt : 05/10/2008 06:24:08PM   WorkSht.DtTm   05/10/2008 06:32:39PM

Main Lab

ELECTROLYTES

Test		Result	Units	Status	Reference Range
Sodium	Conventional	140.30	mEq /l		135.00 - 147.0
	S.I.	140.30	mmol/l		135.00 - 147.00
Potassium	Conventional	4.20	mEq/l		3.30 - 4.80
	S.I.	4.20	mmol/l		3.30 - 4.80
Chloride	Conventional	111.50	mEq/l	H	101.00 - 111.0
	S.I.	111.50	mmol/l		101.00 - 111.00

** End of Report **

DR. T. F. ASHAVAID
Consultant Biochemist
Report Printed On   05-Oct-2008 19:09

P. D. HINDUJA NATIONAL HOSPITAL
& MEDICAL RESEARCH CENTRE
(Established and managed by the National Health & Education Society)

VEER SAVARKAR MARG, MAHIM, MUMBAI - 400 016, INDIA
PHONE : 2445 1515, 2445 2222, 2444 9199 FAX : 2444 9151

DEPARTMENT OF LABORATORY MEDICINE
BIOCHEMISTRY

ORDER NO. : 11705979

HH NO. : 1000298   ADM. NO. : 1086889

NAME   : C K SREEDHARAN

AGE   : 50 YEARS   SEX   : MALE

DATE   : 06/10/2008   LOCATION   : 16S9

REFERRED BY DR.   : ALMEL SACHIN V

Samp. Coll Dt   06/10/2008 03:00:33AM

WorkSht.DtTm   06/10/2008 06:04:41AM

Stat Lab

GENERAL BODY PROFILE

Test		Result	Units	Status	Reference Range	
Fasting Blood Glucose	Conventional	98.00	mg/dl		70.00 -	115.00
	S.I.	5.38	mmol/l		3.85 -	6.33
Sodium	Conventional	141.10	mEq /l		135.00 -	147.0
	S.I.	141.10	mmol/l		135.00 -	147.00
Potassium	Conventional	4.20	mEq/l		3.30 -	4.80
	S.I.	4.20	mmol/l		3.30 -	4.80
Chloride	Conventional	106.10	mEq/l		101.00 -	111.0
	S.I.	106.10	mmol/l		101.00 -	111.00
TCO2	Conventional	26.10	mmol/l		23.00 -	27.00
	S.I.	26.10	mmol/l		23.00 -	27.00
Anion Gap	Conventional	13.10	mEq/l	H	8.00 -	12.00
	S.I	13.10	mmol/l		8.00 -	12.00
Blood Urea Nitrogen	Conventional	5.00	mg/dl		5.00 -	25.00
	S.I.	1.79	mmol/l		1.79 -	8.93
Osmolality (calculated)		278.70	mOsm/l	L	280.00 -	295.00
Creatinine	Conventional	0.80	mg/dl		0.70 -	1.31
	S.I.	70.72	umol/l		61.88 -	115.80

DR. T. F. ASHAVAID

Consultant Biochemist

Report Printed On :   06-Oct-2008 10:06

P. D. HINDUJA NATIONAL HOSPITAL
& MEDICAL RESEARCH CENTRE
(Established and managed by the National Health & Education Society)

VEER SAVARKAR MARG, MAHIM, MUMBAI - 400 016, INDIA
PHONE : 2445 1515, 2445 2222, 2444 9109 FAX : 2444 9151

DEPARTMENT OF LABORATORY MEDICINE
BIOCHEMISTRY

ORDER NO. : 11705979   HH NO. : 1000298   ADM NO. : 1086889

NAME : C K SREEDHARAN   AGE : 50 YEARS   SEX : MALE

DATE : 06/10/2008   LOCATION : 16S9   REFERRED BY DR. : ALMEL SACHIN V

Samp. Coll Dt 06/10/2008 03.00.33AM   WorkSht.DtTm   06/10/2008 06:04:44AM

Stat Lab

GENERAL BODY PROFILE

Test		Result	Units	Status	Reference Range
Calcium	Conventional	8.30	mg/dl		8.00 - 10.40
	S.I.	2.08	mmol/l		2.00 - 2.60
Total Protein	Conventional	5.50	g/dl	L	6.70 - 8.20
	S.I.	55.00	g/l		67.00 - 82.00
Albumin	Conventional	3.20	g/dl	L	3.50 - 5.00
	S.I.	32.00	g/l		35.00 - 50.00
Globulin	Conventional	2.30	g/dl	L	2.60 - 4.10
	S.I.	23.00	g/l		26.00 - 41.00
A/G Ratio		1.40			1.20 - 2.50
Bilirubin(Total)	Conventional	0.70	mg/dl		0.20 - 1.00
	S.I.	11.97	umol/l		3.42 - 17.10
SGOT	Conventional	15.00	U/l		15.00 - 48.00
	S.I.	15.00	IU/l		15.00 - 48.00
SGPT	Conventional	12.00	U/l		10.00 - 40.00
	S.I.	12.00	IU/l		10.00 - 40.00
Alkaline Phosphatase	Conventional	47.00	U/l		40.00 - 120.0
	S.I.	47.00	IU/l		40.00 - 120.00

6/10/08

DR. T. F. ASHAVAID

Consultant Biochemist
Report Printed On :   06-Oct-2008 10:06

P. D. HINDUJA NATIONAL HOSPITAL
& MEDICAL RESEARCH CENTRE

(Established and managed by the National Health & Education Society)

VEER SAVARKAR MARG, MAHIM, MUMBAI - 400 016, INDIA
PHONE : 2445 1515, 2445 2222, 2444 9199 FAX : 2444 9151

DEPARTMENT OF LABORATORY MEDICINE
BIOCHEMISTRY

ORDER NO. : 11705979   HH NO. : 1000298   ADM. NO. : 1086889

NAME : C K SREEDHARAN   AGE : 50 YEARS   SEX   MALE

DATE : 06/10/2008   LOCATION : 16S9   REFERRED BY DR. : ALMEL SACHIN V

Samp. Coll Dt   06/10/2008 03:00:33AM   WorkSht.DtTm   06/10/2008 06:04 44AM

Stat Lab

GENERAL BODY PROFILE

Test	Result		Units	Status	Reference Range	
Gamma G.T.	Conventional	11.00	U/l		0.00 -	50.00
	S.I.	11.00	IU/l		0.00 -	60.00

* * End of Report * *

DR. T. F. ASHAVAID

Consultant Biochemist

Report Printed On   06-Oct-2008 10:06

P. D. HINDUJA NATIONAL HOSPITAL
& MEDICAL RESEARCH CENTRE
(Established and managed by the National Health & Education Society)

VEER SAVARKAR MARG, MAHIM, MUMBAI - 400 016, INDIA
PHONE : 2445 1515, 2445 2222, 2444 9199 FAX : 2444 9151

DEPARTMENT OF LABORATORY MEDICINE
HEMATOLOGY

ORDER NO. : 11711512		HH NO. : 1000298	ADM. NO. 1086889
NAME : C K SREEDHARAN		AGE : 50 YEARS	SEX : MALE
DATE : 07/10/2008	LOCATION : 16S9	REFERRED BY DR. : ALMEL SACHIN V	
Samp. Coll Dt : 07/10/2008 03:24:29AM		WorkSht.DtTm: 07/10/2008 05:29.22AM	

COMPLETE BLOOD COUNT

Test	Result	Units	Abnormality	Reference Range
RED CELL COUNT	3.87	10^12/l	L	4.50 - 6.50
HEMOGLOBIN	10.60	g/dl	L	13.00 - 18.00
HEMATOCRIT	31.40	%	L	40.00 - 54.00
MCV	85.60	fl		76.00 - 96.00
MCH	28.90	pg		27.00 - 32.00
MCHC	33.80	g/dl		30.00 - 35.00
RDW	14.80	%	H	11.50 - 14.50
PLATELET COUNT	310.00	10^9/l		150.00 - 400.00
MPV	9.90	fl		6.80 - 12.60
WBC & DIFF COUNT				
WBC Count	27.34	10^9/l	H	4.00 - 11.00
Diff. WBC Count				
Neutrophils	95.00	%	H	40.00 - 75.00
Eosinophils	0.00	%	L	1.00 - 6.00
Lymphocytes	2.00	%	L	20.00 - 45.00
Monocytes	2.00	%		2.00 - 10.00
Basophils	0.00	%		0.00 - 1.00
Band Cells	1.00	%		

* * End of Report * *

DR. S.KHODAIJI / DR. S GHOSH / DR. A. S. DESHPANDE
Consultant, Hematologist
Report Printed On : 07-Oct-2008 09:49

P. D. HINDUJA NATIONAL HOSPITAL
& MEDICAL RESEARCH CENTRE
(Established and managed by the National Health & Education Society)

VEER SAVARKAR MARG, MAHIM, MUMBAI - 400 016, INDIA
PHONE : 2445 1515, 2445 2222, 2444 9199 FAX : 2444 9151

DEPARTMENT OF LABORATORY MEDICINE
HEMATOLOGY

ORDER NO. : 11742828

NAME : C K SREEDHARAN

DATE : 14/10/2008   LOCATION : 16S9

Samp. Coll Dt : 14/10/2008 03:22:14AM

HH NO. : 1000298   ADM. NO. : 1086889

AGE : 50 YEARS   SEX : MALE

REFERRED BY DR. : ALMEL SACHIN V

WorkSht.DtTm: 14/10/2008 05:18:43AM

COMPLETE BLOOD COUNT

Test	Result	Units	Abnormality	Reference Range	
RED CELL COUNT	2.99	10^12/l	L	4.50 -	6.50
HEMOGLOBIN	8.50	g/dl	L	13.00 -	18.00
HEMATOCRIT	24.90	%	L	40.00 -	54.00
MCV	83.30	fl		76.00 -	96.00
MCH	28.40	pg		27.00 -	32.00
MCHC	34.10	g/dl		30.00 -	35.00
RDW	13.40	%		11.50 -	14.50
PLATELET COUNT	2.00	10^9/l	L	150.00 -	400.00
MPV	10.40	fl		6.80 -	12.60
WBC & DIFF COUNT					
WBC Count	0.03	10^9/l	L	4.00 -	11.00

Comments : WBC: Differential count not possible as counts are very low , few lymphocytes seen
Platelets :Markedly reduced

* * End of Report * *

DR. S.KHODAIJI / DR. S GHOSH / DR. A. S. DESHPANDE
Consultant, Hematologist
Report Printed On : 14-Oct-2008 15:49

P. D. HINDUJA NATIONAL HOSPITAL
& MEDICAL RESEARCH CENTRE
(Established and managed by the National Health & Education Society)

VEER SAVARKAR MARG, MAHIM, MUMBAI - 400 018, INDIA
PHONE : 2445 1515, 2445 2222, 2444 9199 FAX : 2444 9151

DEPARTMENT OF LABORATORY MEDICINE
HEMATOLOGY

ORDER NO. : 11754091   HH NO. : 1000298   ADM. NO. : 1086889

NAME : C K SREEDHARAN   AGE : 50 YEARS   SEX : MALE

DATE : 16/10/2008   LOCATION : 16S9   REFERRED BY DR. : ALMEL SACHIN V

Samp. Coll Dt : 16/10/2008 03:19:05AM   WorkSht DtTm: 16/10/2008 04:19:43AM

COMPLETE BLOOD COUNT

Test	Result	Units	Abnormality	Reference Range	
RED CELL COUNT	3.45	10^12/l	L	4.50 -	6.50
HEMOGLOBIN	9.80	g/dl	L	13.00 -	18.00
HEMATOCRIT	28.80	%	L	40.00 -	54.00
MCV	83.50	fl		76.00 -	96.00
MCH	28.40	pg		27.00 -	32.00
MCHC	34.00	g/dl		30.00 -	35.00
RDW	13.40	%		11.50 -	14.50
PLATELET COUNT	13.00	10^9/l	L	150.00 -	400.00
MPV	9.10	fl		6.80 -	12.60
WBC & DIFF COUNT					
WBC Count	0.16	10^9/l	L	4.00 -	11.00
Diff. WBC Count					
Neutrophils	51.00	%		40.00 -	75.00
Eosinophils	0.00	%	L	1.00 -	6.00
Lymphocytes	45.00	%		20.00 -	45.00
Monocytes	4.00	%		2.00 -	10.00
Basophils	0.00	%		0.00 -	1.00

Comments : Platelets : Markedly reduced.

* * End of Report * *

DR. S.KHODAIJI / DR. S GHOSH / DR. A. S. DESHPANDE
Consultant, Hematologist
Report Printed On : 16-Oct-2008 14:03

P. D. HINDUJA NATIONAL HOSPITAL
& MEDICAL RESEARCH CENTRE
(Established and managed by the National Health & Education Society)

VEER SAVARKAR MARG, MAHIM, MUMBAI - 400 016, INDIA
PHONE : 2445 1515, 2445 2222, 2444 9199 FAX : 2444 9151

DEPARTMENT OF LABORATORY MEDICINE
HEMATOLOGY

ORDER NO. : 11791515	HH NO. : 1000298	ADM. NO. : 1086889
NAME : C K SREEDHARAN	AGE : 50 YEARS	SEX : MALE
DATE : 24/10/2008 LOCATION : 16S9	REFERRED BY DR : ALMEL SACHIN V	
Samp.Coll.Dt : 24/10/2008 04:57:06AM	WorkSht.DtTm: 24/10/2008 07:32:40AM	

COMPLETE BLOOD COUNT

Test	Result	Units	Abnormality	Reference Range
RED CELL COUNT	2.98	10^12/l	L	4.50 - 6.50
HEMOGLOBIN	8.50	g/dl	L	13.00 - 18.00
HEMATOCRIT	25.00	%	L	40.00 - 54.00
MCV	83.90	fl		76.00 - 96.00
MCH	28.50	pg		27.00 - 32.00
MCHC	34.00	g/dl		30.00 - 35.00
RDW	14.00	%		11.50 - 14.50
PLATELET COUNT	9.00	10^9/l	L	150.00 - 400.00
MPV	10.90	fl		6.80 - 12.60
WBC & DIFF COUNT				
WBC Count	6.25	10^9/l		4.00 - 11.00
Diff. WBC Count				
Neutrophils	78.00	%	H	40.00 - 75.00
Eosinophils	4.00	%		1.00 - 6.00
Lymphocytes	11.00	%	L	20.00 - 45.00
Monocytes	5.00	%		2.00 - 10.00
Basophils	0.00	%		0.00 - 1.00
Band Cells	1.00	%		
Metamyelocytes	1.00	%		

Comments : Platelets : Markedly reduced

* * End of Report * *

DR. S.KHODAIJI / DR. S GHOSH / DR. A. S. DESHPANDE
Consultant, Hematologist
Report Printed On : 24-Oct-2008 12:20

P. D. HINDUJA NATIONAL HOSPITAL
& MEDICAL RESEARCH CENTRE
(Established and managed by the National Health & Education Society)

VEER SAVARKAR MARG, MAHIM, MUMBAI - 400 016, INDIA
PHONE : 2445 1515, 2445 2222, 2444 9199 FAX : 2444 9151

DISCHARGE SUMMARY / CARD

Name : C K SREEDHARAN   Age : 50 Y   Sex . M
HH No :1000298   Admission No .1086889
Admission Date :30/09/2008   Discharge Date : 24/10/08
Location :16S9

FINAL DIAGNOSIS:
Autologous stem cell transplant in a case of multiple myeloma.

CHIEF COMPLAINTS AND HISTORY:
50 year old male recently diagnosed multiple myeloma. Presently admitted for Auto stem cell transplant. Treated with 4 cycles of Bortezomab + steroids + Thalidomide. In remission at the time of admission stem cell harvesting done.

PERTINENT PHYSICAL FINDINGS:
On examination G/C - fair
Vitals - stable
Grade I neuropathy present.

COURSE IN WARD:
High dose Melphelan conditional regimen done on D1 on 05.10.2008.
Inj 3 Melphelan 300mg I.V. over 5mins with preconditioning as per the protocol given and antibiotics
Tab Levoflox 500mg od
Tab Septran DS 1bd on Monday and Thursday,
Tab Forcan 200mg od
Tab Acyclovir 200mg 3 times a day
Liquid Wallamycin 30ml bd
Bactroban oint to both nostril twice a day.
Tab Zyloric 100mg 3 times a day
Tab Rantac 150mg twice a day
Tab Stemetil 5mg 2 tab 8 hrly
Tab Ativan 2mg HS
Started with premedication.

Autologous stem cell infusion was done on 06.10.2008 under all aseptic precautions.
Post stem cell transfusion patient developed high creat on day +2.
Reference was given to Dr. J. Kothari. He advised hydration and urine spot protein and creat. However creat settled to 0.2 on its own within 24 hrs.

Patient developed fever on 12.10.2008 and therefore 1st line antibiotics were started. Developed grade 3 mucositis and however patient temp did not respond within 24 hrs and hence Inj Ambisome was added. Daily monitoring of his counts were done.

119

Sreedharan C K

P. D. HINDUJA NATIONAL HOSPITAL
& MEDICAL RESEARCH CENTRE
(Established and managed by the National Health & Education Society)

VEER SAVARKAR MARG, MAHIM, MUMBAI - 400 016, INDIA
PHONE : 2445 1515, 2445 2222, 2444 9199 FAX : 2444 9151

CBC on 20.10.2008:
Hb 9.1　　TLC 2910　　　PLT 13,000　　　Creat 0.4
Alb 2.4　　Rest of the liver profile - normal

24/10/08
Hb -8.5　　　　　TLC – 6250　　　Platelets -9000
1 pint irradiated SDP given today.

TREATMENT AT DISCHARGE:
Tab Levoflox 500mg od
Tab Septran DS 1bd on Monday and Thursday,
Tab Forcan 200mg od
Tab Acyclovir 200mg 3 times a day
Liquid Wallamycin 30ml bd
Bactroban oint to both nostril twice a day
Tab Zyloric 100mg 3 times a day
Tab Rantac 150mg twice a day
Tab Stemetil 5mg 2 tab SOS if nausea, vomiting
Tab Ativan 2mg HS

Patient is advised to follow up on Monday (27/10/08) with Dr Sachin Almel in Onco OPD.

DR. SACHIN ALMEL　　　　　　　DR. URMI
CONSULTANT - ONCOLOGIST　　　REGISTRAR - ONCOLOGY

RE:MRD/vrp/24.10.2008

PLEASE BRING THIS DISCHARGE SUMMARY/CARD FOR FURTHER REFERENCE.
"IN CASE OF EMERGENCY PLEASE REACH CASUALTY IMMEDIATELY"

My CBC and other vital parameters were monitored on a daily basis. While haemoglobin, white blood cells and other blood components showed gradual improvements, platelet count fell to alarming levels. On 19/10/2008, Dr. Sachin Almel informed me that I needed platelet transfusion and asked me to arrange for donors. Platelets from single donor, in medical terminology called as Single Donor Platelets (SDP), was preferable. If patient was unable to find platelet donors, the hospital arranged for platelets, but that could be from multiple donors.

My sister-in-law, Mrs. Priya Murali, who was working with Ms. Rehaja Construction Company, Khar mobilized many platelet donors from her organization. Mr. Panchal, our family friend also brought some donors from 'Gayatri Parivar'. Mr. Panchal's eighteen year old son, Mr. Ankur donated platelets on two occasions.

I received platelet transfusion for the first time on 21/10/2008, fifteen days after stem cell transplant. It was needed because my platelets level had reached very low levels and it showed a rapid reducing trend.

Deepawali festival was on 28/10/2008, and I requested Dr. Sachin Almel to discharge me before the festival, so that I could celebrate the festival at home with my daughters and parents. He agreed, and advised me to come to the hospital frequently till the time platelets count reached minimum threshold limit and stabilized. Dr. Sachin Almel decided to discharge me on 24/10/2008. The CBC was checked on 24/10/2008 and the second platelet transfusion was given on 24/10/2008, late in the evening, before my discharge. I was discharged from the hospital on 24/10/2008, with the advice to come back for a check up on 27/10/2008.

I went to the hospital as advised on 27/10/2008 for check up, and my platelet count was again found very low. The third platelet transfusion was given on 27/10/2008. I was admitted in the day care section of the hospital and was discharged on the same day after the transfusion.

Subsequently I received further platelet transfusions on 07/11/2008, 12/11/2008, 17/11/2008 and for the last time on 28/11/2008. Platelets count stabilized only after the seventh round of platelets transfusion. In addition to platelets, blood transfusions were given on 07/11/2008 and on 28/11/2008, as my haemoglobin level had also gone down.

When I look back and recollect those days it brings unending tears. On each occasion when I needed platelets transfusion, several good Samaritans and noble hearted people, lined up voluntarily. Donors came from far and distant places, waited patiently and donated, expecting nothing in return. There were several unknown strangers, whom I had never met and many did not reveal their identities. Probably I may never meet these good souls again in my life time. Today I am alive and ticking because of the great humanitarian gesture extended by all these known and unknown angels. I whole heartedly pray for their well being and disease free life for them and for their family members.

Purify indoor air naturally:

Usage of activated charcoal as a natural air purifier is an age old practice. In a city like Mumbai, where the humidity levels are quite high, air borne pollutants hang around in the moist air for longer. Keeping activated charcoal helps because it has the ability to dehumidify air.

Coconut shells are one of the most commonly used raw materials for creating activated carbon. Activated carbon filters are easily available in the market. There are millions of pores in a small amount of activated carbon which offers massive surface space for water or air to pass through. This surface space grabs onto toxins and holds them in place, giving activated carbon its fantastic purifying ability.

- Mumbai Mirror dated 28 November, 2017.

Cancer is such an extraordinarily strange unexpected process-some part of your own body growing uncontrollably until it harms you…..

The cancer process can be simplified into three basic levels:

Level I- Initiation of cell damage by carcinogens or procarcinogens.

Level II- Promotion and progression toward a clinically definable cancer state.

Level III- Indisputable cancer and its spread (metastasis) to other areas of the body.

Different factors cause, promote, or maintain the cancer process at each of these levels. Some factors, such as smoking, may play a role at more than one stage.

Any chemical agent that initiates the cancer process is a carcinogen or procarcinogen. All around us in the environment are such initiators as PCBs (polychlorinated biphenyls), diverse pesticides, dioxin, petroleum-based products, cooking and heating fumes, cigarette smoke (both first and second-hand) and ultraviolet (UV) radiation from the Sun. These high-risk initiators might be considered to be over and above cancer-inducing effects of normal metabolism, the pro-oxidant processes that we outlined above in our discussion of free-radical pathology.

- From the book, 'Lower your cancer risk now!'

Rice bran is the new superfood:

Traditionally dismissed as a cheap fibre source, rice bran or the outer coating of rice grain could be the new superfood according to a US study.

A single serving of rice bran delivers more than half of a person's daily requirements of important vitamins such as thiamine, niacin and vitamin B6 which help in energy production and cardiovascular health.

- Times of India, Mumbai edition dated 11 June, 2017.

Walk 25 min a day to cut cancer risk:

Walking for 25 minutes a day can dramatically reduce the risk of dying from cancer, research shows. Two studies have found that regular exercise, such as brisk strolls, can help people after being diagnosed.

One investigation suggested patients who did an average of 25 minutes of moderate-intensity daily exercise were half as likely to die.

In the second probe, 992 people with bowel cancer were assessed over seven years. Compared to those who stuck least to the American Cancer Society guidelines on nutrition and exercise, those who followed them closely had a 42% lower risk of dying.

The advice includes moderate exercise for an average of 22 minutes per day.

- Times of India, Mumbai edition dated 11 June, 2016.

Follow up phase

'Cancer's stronghold is fear. It arrives, announces your death (often with a target date), and clamps itself to your ensuing panic, like a baby to a billowing breast. This is part of what makes cancer so effective. It feeds on your conviction that your days are numbered and the writing is on the wall. Your fear becomes its refuge and your stress its sustenance. It seems to thrive on resignation and despair.

Kill your killer beliefs because they can sap your energy and vitality as surely as your tumours can.'

(The cancer whisperer- Sophe Sabbage , Mumbai Mirror, 9 March, 2017)

My platelets counts stabilized after the seventh platelets transfusion, which was done on 28/11/2008.

Dr. Sachin Almel told me that I need to take Zoldonat injection once in every month for about a year. Zoldonat injection was started from 18/03/2009 and continued up to 06/02/2010, at the frequency of one injection per month.

1	2	3	4	5	6	7	8	9	10	11	12
18 March 2009	15/4	3/5	19/6	16/7	12/8	9/9	7/10	4/11	01/12	6 Jan 2010	6/02

Table 2- Zoldonat administration dates.

Dr. Sachin Almel advised me that henceforth I had to undergo continuous surveillance at regular intervals. Initially I was asked to come for follow up checkups once in every six months.

After seven satisfactory six monthly follow up checkups I was advised to come for a follow up checkup once in a year.

1	2	3	4	5	6	7
06/02/2009	12/08	06/03/2010	07/09	11/03/2011	15/09	05/04/2012

Table 3- Six monthly follow up checkup dates

During the six monthly follow up checkups, the following test were carried out:
1. Bone marrow interpretation;
2. Freelite chains;
3. Beta 2 Microglobulin (B 2 M);
4. CBC;
5. ESR; and
6. Creatinine

The scanned copies of the medical reports of the follow up checkups are attached.

The last bone marrow testing was done on 15/09/2011. Dr. Sachin Almel told me that since other reports were normal, henceforth there was no need for me to undergo six monthly bone marrow tests.

As my six monthly medical reports were consistently normal, after seventh six monthly follow up checkup on 05/04/2012, I was informed that it would be sufficient to undergo follow up checkups once in a year.

All my family members were extremely happy to hear the news.

Since 05/04/2012, I am sincerely and meticulously following medical advice and undergoing the follow up checkups once in a year.

Recent and the last follow up checkup was done on 04/10/2016.

Table 4 - Yearly follow up checkup dates.

1	2	3	4
12/06/2013	08/11/2014	25/07/2015	04/10/2016

During yearly regular checkups following tests were carried out:
1. CBC;
2. Oncoprofile;
3. ESR;
4. Serum Protein Electrophoresis; and
5. Beta 2 Microglobulin (B 2 M)

The scanned copies of the medical reports of the recent follow up checkup done on 04-10-2016 are attached.

Sleep inducing foods:

Sleep disorders are getting bigger and so is the need to sleep better and more peacefully.
Amongst many other wellness practices, one trend that will be big is turning to sleep-savvy food.
Miso soup, oatmeal, pistachios, prunes, chamomile tea are all sleep inducing foods.
- Times of India, Mumbai edition dated 31 December, 2017.

You have over 100 trillion cells in your body. Considering the assault they're under, the remarkable thing about the human body is the complete efficiency with which it will usually suppress cancer. Your body is custom designed to prevent malignancies. It is a cancer-crushing machine.

Yet cancers do start-at the cellular level. Cancer cells are very different from the normal cells in your body. Let me tell you what happens as a cell matures. Fresh, young cells in their immature state have not yet been fitted out to perform necessary activities in the body, they are what physicians call undifferentiated. As these cells, differentiate, they have 'career paths' chosen for them from which, henceforth, they will never deviate.

It is these youthful, undifferentiated cells that most typically become cancerous. As a result, they never do mature-they never take up a 'profession,' they never serve a useful function, they never differentiate. Their job, in fact, is to grow and multiply as part of a rebel cancer colony. In that role, they will bring disorder to your body and, just possibly, terminal chaos.

- From the book –'Lower your cancer risk now!'

P. D. HINDUJA NATIONAL HOSPITAL
& MEDICAL RESEARCH CENTRE
(Established and managed by the National Health & Education Society)

VEER SAVARKAR MARG, MAHIM, MUMBAI - 400 016, INDIA
PHONE : 2445 1515, 2445 2222, 2444 9199 FAX : 2444 9151

DEPARTMENT OF LABORATORY MEDICINE
HEMATOLOGY

ORDER NO. : 17110394

HH NO. : 1000298   ADM. NO. :

NAME : C K SREEDHARAN

AGE : 53 YEARS   SEX : MALE

DATE : 15/09/2011   LOCATION : OPD   REFERRED BY DR. : ALMEL SACHIN V

Samp. Coll Dt : 15/09/2011 03:14:21PM   WorkShl.DtTm : 15/09/2011 03:23:02PM

BONE MARROW INTERPRETATION

BM Smear No. :	322/2011
Cellularity :	Normocellular
M:E Ratio :	1.4 : 1
Erythropoiesis :	There is normoblastic erythroid hyperplasia
Myelopoiesis :	Myeloid cells show normal maturation
Lymphopoiesis :	Lymphoid cells constitute 10% and plasma cells of all nucleate cells
Megakaryopoiesis :	Megakaryocytes appear adequate in number
Impression :	Follow up case of multiple myeloma on treatment showing 1% plasma cells

---

* * End of Report * *

DR. S.KHODAIJI / DR KUNAL SEHGAL/ DR TINA DADU / DR. A. S. DESHPANDE
Consultant, Hematologist
Report Printed On : 16-Sep-2011 17:07

P. D. HINDUJA NATIONAL HOSPITAL
& MEDICAL RESEARCH CENTRE
(Established and managed by the National Health & Education Society)

VEER SAVARKAR MARG, MAHIM, MUMBAI - 400 016, INDIA
PHONE : 2445 1515, 2445 2222, 2444 9199 FAX : 2444 9154

DEPARTMENT OF LABORATORY MEDICINE

HEMATOLOGY

ORDER NO. : 28342928	HH NO. : 1000298	ADM. NO. :
NAME : C K SREEDHARAN	AGE : 58 YEARS	SEX : MALE
DATE : 04/10/2016 LOCATION : OPD	REFERRED BY DR. : ALMEL SACHIN V	
Samp. Coll Dt : 04/10/2016 12:49:57PM	WorkSht.DtTm : 04/10/2016 12:53:36PM	
	Visit Type : ON	

ONCOLOGY PRE-CHEMOTH

Test	Result	Units	Abnormality	Reference Range
RED CELL COUNT	4.65	10^12/l		4.50 - 6.50
HEMOGLOBIN	14.30	g/dl		13.00 - 18.00
HEMATOCRIT	41.80	%		40.00 - 54.00
MCV	89.90	fl		76.00 - 96.00
MCH	30.80	pg		27.00 - 32.00
MCHC	34.20	g/dl		30.00 - 35.00
RDW	12.80	%		11.50 - 14.50
PLATELET COUNT	246.00	10^9/l		150.00 - 400.00
MPV	8.90	fl		6.80 - 12.60
Total WBC Count	6.02	10^9/l		4.00 - 11.00
Neutrophils	47.00	%		40.00 - 75.00
Eosinophils	1.00	%		1.00 - 6.00
Lymphocytes	43.00	%		20.00 - 45.00
Monocytes	9.00	%		2.00 - 10.00
Basophils	0.00	%		0.00 - 1.00
NRBC	0.00	100WBC		

Comments : Automated differential count

** End of Report **

DR. S.KHODAIJI, MD / DR. DIA MANSUKHANI, MD / DR. A. S. DESHPANDE, MD
Consultant, Hematologist
Report Printed On : 04-Oct-2016 16:31

Page 2 of 2
cksiyengar@gmail.com

P. D. HINDUJA NATIONAL HOSPITAL
& MEDICAL RESEARCH CENTRE
(Established and managed by the National Health & Education Society)

VEER SAVARKAR MARG, MAHIM, MUMBAI - 400 016, INDIA
PHONE : 2445 1515, 2445 2222, 2444 9199 FAX : 2444 9151

DEPARTMENT OF LABORATORY MEDICINE

BIOCHEMISTRY

ORDER NO. : 28342928		HH NO. : 1000298	ADM NO. :
NAME : C K SREEDHARAN		AGE : 58 YEARS	SEX : MALE
DATE : 04/10/2016 LOCATION : OPD		REFERRED BY DR. : ALMEL SACHIN V	
SAMP. COLL DT : 04/10/2016 12:49:57PM		WORK SHT.DTTM : 04/10/2016 12:53:36PM	
MAIN LAB		Visit Type : ON	

ONCOLOGY PRE-CHEMOTH

Test		Result	Units	Status	Reference Range
Albumin	Conventional	4.70	g/dl		3.50 - 5.00
Serum Bromocresol Purple	S.I.	47.00	g/l		35.00 - 50.00
SGOT	Conventional	25.00	U/l		15.00 - 48.00
Serum Enzymatic	S.I.	25.00	IU/l		15.00 - 48.00
SGPT	Conventional	34.00	U/l		10.00 - 40.00
Serum Enzymatic	S.I.	34.00	IU/l		10.00 - 40.00
Alkaline Phosphatase	Conventional	43.00	U/l		40.00 - 120.0
Serum Enzymatic	S.I	43.00	IU/l		40.00 - 120.00
LDH	Conventional	154.00	U/L		135.00 - 225.0
Serum Enzymatic	S.I.	154.00	IU/l		135.00 - 225.00
Creatinine	Conventional	0.90	mg/dl		0.70 - 1.31
Serum Jaffe rate	S.I.	79.56	umol/l		61.88 - 115.80
Calcium	Conventional	10.10	mg/dl		8.00 - 10.40
Serum ISE	S.I.	2.53	mmol/l		2.00 - 2.60
Phosphorus	Conventional	4.10	mg/dl		2.50 - 5.00
Serum Phosphomolybdate	S.I.	1.32	mmol/l		0.81 - 1.62

4/10/2016

DR. T. F. ASHAVAID / DR ALPA J DHERAI

Consultant Biochemist

Report Printed On   04-Oct-2016 14:05

cksiyengar@gmail.com
Page 1 of 2

P. D. HINDUJA NATIONAL HOSPITAL
& MEDICAL RESEARCH CENTRE

(Established and managed by the National Health & Education Society)

VEER SAVARKAR MARG, MAHIM, MUMBAI - 400 016, INDIA
PHONE : 2445 1515, 2445 2222, 2444 9199, FAX : 2444 0151

DEPARTMENT OF LABORATORY MEDICINE

HEMATOLOGY

ORDER NO. :	28342928		HH.NO. : 1000298	ADM. NO. :	
NAME	: C K SREEDHARAN		AGE : 58 YEARS	SEX : MALE	
DATE	: 04/10/2016	LOCATION : OPD	REFERRED BY DR. : ALMEL SACHIN V		
Samp. Coll Dt : 04/10/2016 12:49:57PM			WorkSht.DtTm : 04/10/2016 12:53:36PM		
			Visit Type : ON		

Test	Result	Units	Abnormality	Reference Range
ESR	10.00	mm/hr		0.00 - 10.00

SKhodai

DR. S.KHODAIJI, MD / DR. DIA MANSUKHANI, MD / DR. A. S. DESHPANDE, MD
Consultant, Hematologist
Report Printed On   04-Oct-2016 16:31

Page 1 of 2
cksiyengar@gmail.com

P. D. HINDUJA NATIONAL HOSPITAL
& MEDICAL RESEARCH CENTRE
(Established and managed by the National Health & Education Society)

VEER SAVARKAR MARG, MAHIM, MUMBAI - 400 016, INDIA
PHONE : 2445 1515, 2445 2222, 2444 9199 FAX : 2444 9151

DEPARTMENT OF LABORATORY MEDICINE
BIOCHEMISTRY

ORDER NO :- 28342928	H.H NO :- 1000298	ADM.NO: -
NAME-: C.K.SREEDHARAN	AGE :- 58	SEX :- M
DATE :- 05/10/2016	LOCATION:-OPD	REF BY:- DR.ALMEL S.

Serum Protein Electrophoresis

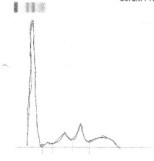

Reference Range

T.Protein -: 7.4   g/dl   6.7 - 8.2 g/dl

A/G Ratio-: 1.78   1.2 - 2.5

Globulin -: 2.7   g/dl   2.6 - 4.1 g/dl

Fractions	%	Ref. %	g/dl	Ref. g/dl
Albumin	64.0	60.0 - 71.0	4.7	3.5 - 5.0
Alpha 1	2.2	1.4 - 2.9	0.2	0.1 - 0.4
Alpha 2	9.8	7.0 - 11.0	0.7	0.4 - 1.2
Beta	11.5	8.0 - 13.0	0.9	0.5 - 1.1
Gamma	12.5	9.0 - 16.0	0.9	0.5 - 1.6

Comments : The result interpretations are based on % reference ranges & not on g/dl.

Extended comment -: interpretation : Protein electrophoresis is within normal limits.M band absent.

5/10/2016

DR.T.F.ASHAVAID/ DR.A.J.DHERAI
Consultant Biochemist

The present phase

'Nothing is more important than your peace and happiness in the here and now.
One day you will lie like a dead body and no longer be able to touch the beauty of a flower.
Make good use of your time.'
                                            - Thich Nhat Hanh

From March 2008 to April 2009 I did not take up any consultancy work due to my preoccupation with the treatment. I was also mentally and physically worn out and was not in a position to take up any consultancy assignment.

Whatever little I had managed to save, was spent on my treatment. As I had already borrowed substantially from my close relatives, I didn't feel like going back to them for more financial support. With no other income, life was miserable. My wife somehow managed to run the household. My daughters were aware of the family condition and helped in cutting down the expenses to a great extent. Those were the dreadful days and I really don't want to think about those wretched days. I am also extremely thankful to the proprietor of the 'Bhavani Stores', the provisional store near my house, from where I used to buy monthly provisions. The proprietor of the Bhavani Stores was aware of my plight, and allowed me to settle my provision bills as per my convenience.

Consultancy job market had hit a bad patch and from 2007 onwards, I did not get enough consultancy assignments. The future prospects of getting regular consultancy assignments appeared bleak and uncertain.

Also I could not effectively follow up with several prospective leads in the last one year due to preoccupation with my treatment.

Along with my consultancy work, I also used to visit Pillai Institute of Management Studies and Research (PIMSR), New Panvel, a leading and reputed management institute in Navi Mumbai area as a visiting / guest faculty. I was a visiting faculty of PIMSR right from the year 2003, except for two years 2007 and 2008. I could make an entry into PIMSR as a visiting faculty due to Dr. R Chandran, whom I met in one of the training sessions at Regional Staff College, Punjab National Bank and my Punjab National Bank friend Dr. Vijayaragavan.   Dr. Vijayaragavan was transferred from Nagpur to Regional Staff College of Punjab National Bank at CBD Belapur. Dr. Vijayaragavan took sabbatical break from Punjab National Bank and joined PIMSR as Dean.

While I was recuperating, I had plenty of time to think about my future career options. My consultancy business was not doing well for the last couple of years and there was uncertainty in earning a decent income. The earning was also erratic. I faced acute financial crisis and I needed a regular income. My family members were also very keen on my taking up a regular job. After a lot of thinking, consultation and deliberation I decided to take up a career in teaching management students, which I was already doing as a visiting faculty.

I consulted Dr. Vijayaragavan and requested him to help me to join as a faculty in PIMSR. Dr. Vijayaragavan informed me that PIMSR was on a faculty recruitment drive and advised me to apply for a faculty position.

Dr, R Chandran, the then Director of PIMSR and Dr. Vijayaragavan knew about my teaching ability and they had no hesitation in recommending me to Dr. K M Vasudevan Pillai, the CEO of Pillai Group of Institutions. I requested for an adjunct faculty position, which required committing three days in a week to PIMSR. This arrangement gave me flexibility to engage in my consultancy work on the remaining days, thereby ensuring at least some steady income.

I worked as an adjunct faculty at PIMSR from June 2009 to December 2009. I did not get any significant consultancy assignments during this period. The prospects of getting any consultancy projects in future also appeared bleak. I decided to take up a full time teaching job in management, as I had already established a foothold in teaching. I expressed my desire to become a full time teaching faculty at PIMSR to Dr. R Chandran and Dr. Vijayaragavan. They also gracefully agreed and made me a full time faculty at PIMSR, New Panvel with effect from 01 January, 2010.

Now it is the appropriate time to write about Dr. K M Vasudevan Pillai, the founder and the Chief Executive Officer of Pillai Group of

Institutions, comprising of 48 institutions. Dr. K M Vasudevan Pillai is an incomparable educationist the country has ever produced and is a great visionary of par excellence. He has built up a massive educational empire within a short span of thirty years from a very humble beginning. Today there are about 3500 faculty working and about 40,000 students studying in various group institutions. Dr. Vasudevan Pillai is a living legend and a great source of inspiration for many of his admirers.

I am emotionally attached to PIMSR, for several reasons. This is the place where I commenced my teaching career and PIMSR gave me an opportunity to rebuild my career, when I was mentally and financially devastated. My first daughter, Saranya did BE-IT in Pillai College of Engineering, a group institution, and she got campus placement in Infosys. My second daughter, Suchitra studied diploma in computer science in Pillai Polytechnic, a group institution. After completing Diploma in Computer Science, she pursued BE in Computer Science from the same Pillai College of Engineering and she also got campus placement in Capgemini. I am greatly indebted to Dr. K M Vasudevan Pillai, the architect of Mahatma Education Society.

I have shared each and every detail about myself without suppressing or exaggerating any of the fact as truly as possible. Earlier, I had mentioned about the three big blunders that I had committed in my life. I also have three big regrets in my life, which will haunt me for the rest of my life:

1.   Even though I have the best possible qualifications, industry experience and exposure, talent and capability to reach higher echelons of the industry, I failed and could not make it big and noteworthy. I failed to exploit the chances and other opportunities that came my way to the best of my advantage;

2.   The second regret is not managing my finances prudently and wisely; and

3.   The most painful regret is the misunderstanding that crept between me and once my best friend, Dr. Vijayaragavan. I tried to be his true friend by giving some unsolicited bitter feedback about himself and his questionable style of functioning, which he construed as back-stabbing. One treacherous, evil and self serving sycophant ensured that we never made up with each other and drifted apart permanently. My real regret is that Dr. Vijayaragavan became a puppet and could not distinguish between a real friend and

a foe. I only like to remember the best times we spent together. I sincerely pray God Almighty for his all round well being.

Medical science categorically proclaims that till now there is no proven cure for multiple myeloma, but it can be treated successfully, there by extending the life span of the patient. It is also said that multiple myeloma will relapse after some years of remission. This remission period may vary from patient to patient. The good news is that, there are patients who have survived beyond ten years.

I would like to strongly advice all multiple myeloma patients and survivors not to worry about the relapse of the disease, which may happen in near future. Let us think of each surviving day as a bonus and a gift of God and try to extract as much as possible from the living days. Let us all develop a strong will and the determination to survive and face the challenges of life as it unfolds. Let us take the monster cancer by the horn and fight to overpower and subdue the dreaded demon.

Can the immune system be rejuvenated to function at a higher, more optimal and balanced level? The good news is that the answer is yes, and a more responsive immune system can add years to your life. As we have seen many of the chronic, age-accelerating diseases such as cancer, can be linked to an immune system that has gone awry. 'Failure of immune function is what tends to kill you as you get older,' says Elmer Cranton, MD. 'If you live to be 120, it will be largely because your immune system demonstrates a superb capacity to deal with the insults of the daily living.'

Immune function and longevity are closely linked. Not only does a robust immune system lessen the likelihood of developing chronic diseases, infections, and other immune-related diseases, but it also enhances DNA replication, insulin sensitivity, and normal thyroid hormone levels, all of which are factors influencing life expectancy. While immune balancing may not allow us to routinely live past our predicted maximum life span of 120 years, it is certain to add years of healthy life we would otherwise not enjoy.

- Book on- 'Longevity- An Alternative Medicine Definitive Guide.'

Immune system

'You gain strength, courage, and confidence by every experience in which you really stop to look fear in the face. You are able to say to yourself, 'I lived through this horror; I can take the next thing that comes along.'

-Eleanor Roosevelt

The very utterance of the word 'cancer' instills fear and dejection in the minds of the people. Surgery, chemotherapy and radiation are a few limited treatment options which may prolong the life of a patient. The possibility of a long term disease free period is really lies with the immune system which is capable of destroying new cancer cell formation.

I have already emphasized that the cancer disease itself is not totally responsible for the death of the patient. The patient also plays a significant role in one's early death. The patient often surrenders to fate and gives up the will to fight the disease head on. In most of the cases, the patient develops a defeatist attitude and gives up living a normal and healthy life. Many a time, the relatives and the friends also add to the gloomy situation by sympathizing and showing pity.

Medicines and regular follow up checks alone may not guarantee good quality life and longevity. It is not that those are not important. They are an integral part of the remaining life time of the survivor. In addition to these, the patient has to adopt a healthy life style and develop a positive attitude.

Human body is very sophisticated and it is created with a lot of complexity. Even the so called advanced medical sciences which boast to have complete knowledge about the human anatomy, may not have fully understood the complexicities. It is also impossible for advanced medical science to come out with a perfect and complete cure for each and every disease.

Human body is self sustaining and is designed with the capability to take care of itself against any type of disease. It is equipped with a powerful self defense mechanism, capable of fighting off any disease, including the dreaded, often incurable cancer. Nature expects human body to protect itself and take care of itself, without any external assistance. All that really required to fight any disease is nothing but a strong and powerful immune system, which the human body is endowed with. I will discuss some proven and widely practiced methods to improve immunity.

The immune system present in the human body protects the body against the disease or other potentially damaging foreign bodies. When functioning properly, the immune system identifies and attacks a variety of threats like viruses, bacteria and parasites, while distinguishing them from body's own healthy tissue.

The immune system is made up of different organs, cells and proteins. Like the nervous system, it is the most complex system that the human body has. The lymphatic system aids the immune system in removing and destroying waste, debris, dead blood cells, pathogens, toxins and cancer cells.

The lymphatic system consists of bone marrow, spleen, thymus and lymph nodes.

Bone marrow produces white blood cells or leukocytes.

Spleen is the largest lymphatic organ in the body containing white blood cells that fight infection or disease.

Thymus is where T-cells mature. T-cells help destroy infected or cancerous cells.

Lymph nodes produce and store cells that fight infection and disease.

Lymphocytes and leukocytes are small white blood cells that play a large role in defending the body against the disease.

Two types of lymphocytes are: B-cells, which make antibodies that attack bacteria and toxins, and T-cells, which help destroy infected or cancerous cells.

Leukocytes are white blood cells that identify and eliminate pathogens.

Immune system plays a vital role in fighting cancer. The immune system can find and attack tumour cell. When this function breaks down it causes cancers and tumours to develop.

Since my treatment that is for the last eight years, I am researching on natural cure and healing system. In India there are many well researched and highly effective natural ways of treating body through herbs, food, yoga, meditation and other practices which are in tune and harmony with nature as well as with the human body.

I once again reiterate that I am neither advocating nor recommending natural healing practices as an alternate cure. The patient's doctor / consultant is best equipped to decide the course of treatment. These are only suggestions, which may be considered along with the ongoing treatment. I strongly recommend the patient to consult the attending doctor, before attempting any of these suggestions.

At this juncture it is necessary to understand free radicals, antioxidants and carotenoids as they play bad and good roles in connection with prevention of diseases.

Free radicals

While converting food to energy, human body generates hundreds of substances called as 'free radicals'. Other free radicals enter the human body from the food or breathed in from air and some are generated by the sunlight's action on the skin and eye. The free radical molecules are missing an electron in their outer shell, and these molecules will do anything to neutralize this unstable position, including stealing electrons from body's cellular structure. Such cellular stealing may damage DNA, proteins and cell membranes. When these cells are damaged, body is damaged, creating foundation for disease and accelerating aging process. The free radicals damage the cells in the body constantly.

The free radical destroys whatever it comes into contact. If it is a cell wall, cell dies. If it is a DNA, it causes a mutation-which may lead to many diseases, especially cancer.

The free radicals exist only for a fraction of a second, but even during such a short duration of existence, they cause serious structural damage to the cells. Once a molecule is oxidized by the free radical, it often starts a chain reaction of oxidation until an antioxidant can stop it. Scientific studies have established that the process of aging and almost every disease that affects the body is caused due to the damage inflicted by the free radicals on the body.

The extent of damage that the free radicals cause on a particular site of a human body determines the type of disease the person may get. If there is more free radical damage to the blood vessels, the person may get heart disease. If there is more free radical damage to the eyes, the person may get cataracts. If there is more free radical damage to the brain, the person may get Alzheimer's. If there is more free radical damage to the breast tissue, the person may get breast cancer and so on.

Antioxidants

If free radicals are deadly villains, antioxidants can be hailed as superheroes. The antioxidants protect the human body from the free radicals. These are molecules which safely interact with the free radicals and terminate chain reaction before the vital molecules are damaged.

Although there are several enzyme systems within the body that disarm the free radicals, the principle antioxidants are Vitamin-E, beta carotene, Vitamin-C and Selenium.

Overall health benefits of antioxidants are limitless. They greatly support the immune system.

When antioxidants neutralize the free radicals by donating an electron particle, they are left with a new problem. The antioxidants are now missing an electron and have become free radicals themselves. This is the reason why free radicals and antioxidants must go hand in hand. Body can't manufacture these antioxidants, so they must be supplied through the diet.

It is necessary to clearly understand one aspect. In theory, the antioxidants have the potential to improve or prevent a number of chronic diseases. But consuming them also does not guarantee prevention or cure for all the diseases. Including antioxidants in the diet is recommended but they are not the magical solution for all the diseases, which they are sometimes hyped to be.

Carotenoids

They are chemically related to Vitamin-A, the most important vitamin for the functioning of immune system.

Types of carotenoids:
1. Beta Carotene, and
2. Lycopene

Beta Carotene: It is one of the important carotenoids and in addition to its convertibility to Vitamin A; it is also an antioxidant, which stimulates the T-Cells in the immune system.

The T-Cells remove invaders from the body. Beta Carotene is abundantly found in carrots.

Lycopene: It is found in tomatoes, carrots, apricots and watermelon. The studies have shown that the levels of prostate cancer are being reduced dramatically with higher intakes of lycopene containing substances. It is also found that a person who eats 10 servings of tomato based food per week reduces risk of prostate cancer by about 45%.

Cooked tomatoes are better than raw tomatoes. Digestive system can extract only a limited amount of lycopene from fresh tomatoes. Research has found that lycopene also protects against cancer of mouth, pharynx, esophagus, stomach, colon, and rectum.

A phytonutrient rich diet, vitamins, minerals, a reasonable exercise regime and avoidance of excessive stress can strengthen the immune system. The beneficial effects and impact of all these on human immune system are discussed in this section.

Vital Vitamins

Vitamin A (Beta-carotene, Retinol and Alpha- carotene)

A deficiency of this vitamin causes night-blindness, dry skin, weakened immunity and can also affect growth and reproduction. A new study has found that intake of this vitamin could help treat several types of cancers due to its ability to control malignant cells. The new study says that Vitamin A can be used as a new anticancer treatment and advice people to ensure to include adequate levels of this vitamin in diets.

It is found in carrots, oranges, pumpkin and egg yolks, in organ meats like liver, cod liver oil and butter.

Vitamin B1 (Thiamine)

A deficiency of this vitamin causes beriberi; a potentially life threatening disease and can also cause Korsakoff's syndrome- a brain disorder.
It is found in legumes, beef, nuts, pork, cereals and yeast.

Vitamin B 2 (Riboflavin)

A deficiency of this vitamin causes low immunity and a drop in energy levels. It helps in nerve development, blood cell development and regulation of certain hormones.
It is found in spinach, mushrooms, yogurt and milk

Vitamin B 3(Niacin)

A deficiency of this vitamin causes Pellagra which is characterized by symptoms such as scaly skin, digestive problems and problems of nervous system.
Insufficient consumption of Vitamin B 3 can also contribute to dementia.
It is found in rice bran, fish (especially tuna), peanuts and broccoli.

Vitamin B 5 (Pantothenic acid)

A deficiency of this Vitamin causes fatigue, insomnia, irritability and depression.
It is found in avocados, sunflower seeds, mushrooms, yogurt, chicken and chicken liver.

Vitamin B 6 (Pyridoxine)

A deficiency of this Vitamin causes swings, anxiety and confusion. It could also impede blood cell formation. It also helps in building immunity
It is found in sunflower seeds, spinach, dried prunes, bananas, and avocados.

Vitamin B 7 (Biotin)

A deficiency of this Vitamin causes anaemia and hair loss / baldness. It is found in eggs, soy milk, and organ meats.

Vitamin B 9 (Folic acid, folacin)

A deficiency of this Vitamin causes neural tube defects. It is important during pregnancy.

It is found in dark green leafy vegetables, citrus fruits, avocado and lentils.

Vitamin B 12 (Cyanocobalamin, Cobalamin)

A deficiency of this Vitamin causes heart problems and brain / nerve damage and fatigue.

It is found in fish, poultry, milk and eggs. Vegetarian diets don't usually contain this Vitamin.

Vitamin C

It helps in the manufacture of collagen, which is necessary for tissue repair. It keeps the immune and nervous systems healthy by strengthening blood vessels. A deficiency of this Vitamin causes scurry which is characterized by bleeding and swollen gums. Insufficient Vitamin C also leads to low immunity levels and dry hair. Vitamin C helps to strengthen the immune system. The best sources of Vitamin C are citrus fruits, gooseberries, sprouts, strawberries, kiwi, bell peppers, dark green vegetables, and capsicum. It is a little known fact that capsicum is one of the richest sources of Vitamin C.

Vitamin D

Sunshine is the best source of this Vitamin. It is essential for bone development. A deficiency is marked by brittle bones and conditions such as rickets. It can also cause bone softening.

Studies have found that exposure to sunshine increases production of nitric acid, which dilates the arteries. The Vitamin D produced by the skin strengthens bones with calcium and also lowers blood pressure, thereby reducing the risk of stroke. Vitamin D improves Calcium absorption by the body.

Sunlight is a natural source and a powerful source of Vitamin D3. The only apparent indicator of a Vitamin D3 deficiency is severe bone pain. Vitamin D3 is both a vitamin and a hormone. It acts as a vitamin when it binds with calcium for proper absorption. Humans can't absorb calcium without adequate amount of Vitamin D3.

Vitamin D3 promotes bone health, controls immune system, increases neuro-muscular function, and protects the brain against toxic chemicals.

This Vitamin is also important for activating human defenses. The Immune system's killer cells, called T-cells, rely on Vitamin D to become active and remain dormant and unaware of the possibility of threat from an infection or pathogen if Vitamin D is lacking in the blood.

This vitamin is found in cheese and egg yolk, but mainly sunshine.

Excessive use of sun-screen hinders body's capacity to develop Vitamin D.

Vitamin E (Alpha-Tocopherol)

This Vitamin helps the body to absorb Vitamin A and to make red blood cells. It's a powerful antioxidant so a deficiency would cause a drop in immunity and the skin would get dry.

It is found in green leafy vegetables, spinach, broccoli, sunflower seeds, nuts, kiwi and avocado.

Vitamin K (Phytonadione)

This Vitamin is essential for blood clotting and its deficiency causes easy bleeding. It binds calcium to the bones.

It is found in spinach, cauliflower, greens, broccoli, cabbage and turnips.

Vitamin B 6, Vitamin A, Vitamin D, folic acid, iron and trace elements like selenium and zinc also help in building immunity.

Essential elements

Calcium

Deficiency causes osteoporosis and osteoporosis conditions that are related to the bones. It can also cause hypocalcaemia which is characterized by brittle bones and muscles that don't contract properly.

It is found in milk and milk products. The best source for calcium is nachni (ragi), a type of millet. Almonds, fish and broccoli are also rich sources of calcium.

Copper

Copper works with iron to make red blood cells and a deficiency of copper causes anaemia, leukopenia (low white blood cell count) and myelodysplasia, in which the immature blood cells in bone marrow do not become healthy blood cells.
It is found in dark green leafy vegetables like spinach, nuts, oysters and shellfish.

Iodine

Deficiency may cause extreme fatigue, weight gain, puffiness of the face, constipation and impaired immunity. It is found in meat, egg yolk, dark green vegetables, nuts and legumes.

Iron

Iron is an essential mineral stored by the body in red blood cells. A deficiency of this will cause anaemia and renders individuals susceptible to infection.
It is found in pumpkin seeds, nuts, and dark green vegetables.

Magnesium

It is vital for a healthy nervous system, for the formation of healthy bones and teeth.
It is found in dry fruits, leafy vegetables and dark chocolate.

Manganese

Deficiency limits production of collagen, which affects body's capacity to heal wounds.
It is found in spinach, pineapple, pumpkin seeds and brown rice.

Potassium
A deficiency can cause hypokalemia (a serious electrolyte imbalance), weakness due to dehydration / diarrhoea and sweating. Those who wish to keep their blood pressure in check can benefit from potassium. It is found in avocados, spinach, coconut water and bananas.

Phosphorous

It helps to keep the bones and teeth strong and healthy.
It is found in dairy products, fish, meat, whole grains and nuts.

Selenium

It prevents degenerative conditions including cancer, inflammatory diseases, cardiovascular disease and neurological diseases. Deficiency weakens the immune system and causes thyroid dysfunction and infertility in men and women.
It is found in brazil nuts, beef, egg and chicken.

Sodium

It works with chloride and bicarbonate to balance positive and negative ions in the body. Deficiency will cause cramps, fluid shifts and acid-base imbalance.
It is found in common salt and processed food.

Zinc

It helps the body to heal the wounds internally. Deficiency will cause reduced immunity and delay in wound healing. It promotes a strong immune system by revitalizing thymus gland and its production of white blood cells.

It is found in chickpeas, pumpkin seeds, mushrooms, chicken and lamb.

Dietary recommendations to boost immunity

Increase protein intake

People who are vegetarians generally have problem with adequate intake of proteins. They need to make a conscious effort to increase the intake of milk, curds, paneer, cheese, soya bean, eggs etc.

Regular intake of nuts

Consume walnuts, almonds, cashew, and peanuts in restricted amounts.

Coarse cereals

Opt for millets, blend of wheat and soya, wheat and chana, breakfast cereals based on oats, soya or wheat.

Get Omega 3 fatty acids

Include flax seeds, walnuts, methi (fenugreek) leaves, fish etc.

Increase intake of anti-oxidants

Ensure intake of Vitamin C, Vitamin E, beta-carotene, minerals like zinc, selenium etc.

Get the lycopene

It is a powerful anti-oxidant found in tomatoes. Cook tomatoes, make a thick soup without straining or make a paste. Doing so improves concentration and availability of this anti-oxidant.

Liver and its function

Unlike other organs-heart, lungs and the digestive tract, which basically do the same job over and over, liver is one organ which does about 400 different jobs, at least doing 10 jobs at the same time. It is also the largest organ in the human body.

Among all important functions, it is responsible for disposing off bodily wastes and decides how to process thousands of unnatural bodily chemicals that body is exposed to. Our body is exposed to cancer-causing toxic substances, throughout the life time. Liver deals with toxins and gets them out of the body.

Broccoli, spinach, strawberries, raspberries, grapes and walnuts are good detoxification promoters. All cruciferous vegetables, green tea and turmeric also help in detoxification. Phytonutrients will also help liver to perform its function satisfactorily. A well functioning liver is essential to fight against cancer.

Liver cleaning

Periodic liver cleaning practice can help prevent an excess build-up of toxins in liver. Liver flushes can be used to eliminate wastes from the body, increase bile flow and improve overall liver health and function.

Preparation of liver flush

Squeeze enough fresh lemons to produce one cup of juice. Add water to dilute the juice, but the sourer it tastes, better it will perform as a liver cleanser. Lemon is an excellent stimulant for liver, and it dissolves uric acid and other toxins. Freshly squeezed orange and grape juices may also be used, provided they are blended with some lemon juice.

To the citrus juice mixture add the juice of 1-2 cloves of garlic, freshly squeezed in a garlic press and a small quantity of freshly grated raw ginger juice. Add one tablespoon of extra virgin olive oil to the juice mixture. Thoroughly mix the composite juice mixture.

Now the liver flush is ready and is best taken in the morning, preferably after doing some stretching exercises.

Do not eat anything, for one hour following the flush. After an hour, take two cups of herbal tea. Liver flush can be done twice a year.

Recent study has found that fat cells may affect cancer development. Studies have shown several ways that fat contributes to carcinogenesis. For example, obesity increases risk of inflammation, which has long been associated with cancer.

Obesity is also believed to affect cancer cell metabolism and immune clearance, all of which can contribute to the growth and spread of tumours.

(Source: Mumbai Mirror dated 04 September, 2017)

Almost 80% of cervical cancer patients are diagnosed in stage 3-4 in India, but the west has almost eradicated this cancer due to regular pap smear tests. Given India's population, it is impossible to scan everybody. Self-breast exams and clinical exams involving community workers or ancillary health professionals are hence crucial.

Tata Memorial, the country's top cancer-care facility, treats around 62,000 new patients from various cities, towns and villages every year and also attends to 4.5 lakh follow-up cases annually. It provides free or highly subsidized treatment in majority of the cases. But the huge workload invariably leads to a long waitlist despite the best efforts of doctors and the staff.

About 30 to 40 people are always found camping outside the hospital every day. Now, the hospital is planning to create a dharmashala (shelter) to house outstation patients and their kin.

Eat nuts for good health:

Nuts are among the healthiest foods one can eat. They are high in fibre, loaded with the antioxidant vitamin E, magnesium and copper, and are a good source of protein that is very high in amino acid called arginine, which helps lower cholesterol and relaxes blood vessels.

A study in the journal BMC Medicine found that eating 28 gms of nuts daily cuts the risk of coronary heart disease by 30%, cancer by 15%, respiratory disease by about a half, and diabetes by nearly 40%.

It is advised to have mixed nuts or have them all by rotation.

References

1. http://www.livescience.com/38028-how-the-human-body-s-immune-system-works

2. http://www.lymphnotes.com/article.php/id/151/)

3. http://www.pharmacytimes.com/publications/issue/2013/january2013/fighting-free-radicals-do-you-need-antioxidants.

4. The Times of India, Mumbai edition dated 30 August, 2009.

5. Mumbai Mirror dated 20 February, 2017.

6. 'Longevity- An alternate medicine definitive guide' – W Lee Cowden & Others.

The gift of nature

'Let food be thy medicine, and
Medicine be thy food.'

-Hyppocrates, the father of western medicine

'Nature heals and the doctor sends the bill,' Mark Twain once remarked. This comment may be a wry observation of a simple fact, but carries an important message. Nature has a remarkable ability to cure human body, naturally.

The cancer fighting phytonutrients are found in abundance in plant kingdom. Phytonutrients are powerful when consumed in sufficient quantity. Phytonutrients are found in fruits, herbs and vegetables. All most all fruits and vegetables have at least a few protective natural chemicals embedded in them.

This section covers the beneficial effects of phytonutrients.

Vegetables

Bitter gourd (Karela)

It contains twice the calcium of spinach, twice the potassium of banana and twice the beta- carotene of broccoli. It is also an excellent source of dietary fiber. Antimicrobial and antioxidant properties of bitter gourd juice can treat blood disorders, remove toxins from blood and purify it. It helps to build immunity.

It improves blood circulation throughout the body. It can prevent cancer cells from multiplying and can even inhibit the growth of cancerous cells in the body.

Bottle gourd

It is regarded as one of the healthiest veggies. It has fewer calories with no fat and contains essential vitamins and minerals like Vitamin C, Vitamin B, Vitamin K, Vitamin A, Vitamin E, iron, folate, potassium and manganese. Ayurveda recommends this vegetable for reducing fat. It helps to maintain a healthy heart and brings down bad cholesterol levels. Juice is also beneficial for diabetic patients as it stabilizes blood sugar level and maintains blood pressure.

Juice should always be consumed fresh. Peel and gourd and try a bit of flesh before blending, it shouldn't taste bitter. If it does, discard it. Also, it is advised to have the juice alone and not mix with other vegetables. However, amla, ginger, fresh mint leave and some rock salt can be added to spruce up flavour.

Broccoli

It is one of the world's top 10 superfoods. It is one of the most nutrient-rich foods in the world. It is packed with nutrients to fight arthritis, boost cardiovascular health and immune system, and build bones. Its biggest health benefit, of course, is that it can help prevent cancer. It has properties that alleviate all the problems related to cancer.

How to consume- One fundamental rule about broccoli is to avoid cooking it. Keep the vegetable as fresh and crunchy as possible, as cooking may take away its nutrients. Boiling reduces the levels of anti-cancer compounds. It is best to steam, microwave, stir-fry or simply eat it raw. Steaming broccoli for 3-4 minutes is recommended to maximize anti-cancer compound sulforaphane. Steaming broccoli increases its concentration of cancer-fighting compounds, while boiling lowers these levels.

Summing up:
-    Broccoli is capable of DNA repair in cells and is capable of blocking the growth of cancer cells;
-    It contains multiple nutrients with potent anti-cancer properties, such as dindolylmethane and small amounts of selenium. It also contains the compound glucoraphanin, which can be processed into anti-cancer compound sulforaphane;
-    Fiber benefits the body's detoxification system; and
-    A single serving provides more than 30 mg of Vitamin C and a half-cup provides 52 mg of Vitamin C.

Beetroots

It is a cleansing agent that detoxifies organs such as kidney, gall bladder and liver in the body. It helps to increase blood cell count and does miracles for anaemic people. Best way to consume beetroot is through beetroot juice as it is low on calories and high on fibers which provides relief from constipation as well as prevention from Alzheimer's and cancer.

Cabbage

It contains sulforaphane- which inhibits and fights cancer cells.

Cauliflower

It is rich in antioxidants. It contains sulforaphane, a sulphur compound that kills cancer stem cells and slows down tumour growth.

Cucumber

It is loaded with potassium. Electrolyte controls heart rate by lowering the effects of sodium.

Curry leaves

It restores hormone imbalance and prevents aging.

Drumstick (Moringa)

Every part of the tree- leaves, flowers, and seeds- is packed with nutrition and can be used to cure various health problems. It is more potent than any other superfoods.

The leaves are the best part of the plant because that is where high levels of vitamins like C, A, and B are present. It gives more calcium than milk, more vitamin C than oranges, more potassium than bananas and more iron than spinach.

Green chilies

Chilies both red and green are rich sources of Vitamin C. It is a powerful antioxidant. It can improve immunity and prevent cancer.

Lettuce

It is a rich source of Vitamin K, which promotes increase in bone mass.

Mushroom

Shiitake mushrooms are found to strengthen immunity. They have been highly valued as both, food and medicine, since ancient times. Traditional Chinese physicians believed the forest mushrooms also had the power to charge the 'Ki' or 'life force' and to promote longevity. Shiitake mushrooms are also a rich source of Vitamin B 12 (this not available in vegetables), riboflavin, niacin, copper, selenium, zinc, dietary fiber and enzymes. They also contain ergosterol, which converts to Vitamin D in the body, and an active compound called lentinan, a polysaccharide that strengthens immune system.

To enjoy the health benefits of shiitake mushrooms, soak 1-2 shiitake mushrooms in water for 10-12 minutes, then,
boil these in 2 cups of water for 20 minutes. Drink half a cup at a time.

Oats

It is good for people who have various vitamin and mineral deficiencies. It helps to boost metabolism and is rich in silicon which helps to renew bones and connective tissue. It restores nervous system, strengthens spleen and pancreas.

Onion

Onions are a rich source of quercertin, a plant flavonoid that fights free radicals.

Pudina (mint leaves)

It is packed with antioxidants and menthol. It soothes the muscles of the stomach, and reduces indigestion, acidity and flatulence.

Radish

It contains phyto-chemicals and anthocyanins that fight cancer

Spinach

It increases red blood cells count in the body. These cells are responsible for carrying oxygen to and fro from lungs to the body. Also contains calcium and zinc, which are needed for strong bones.

Sweet potatoes

It is rich in fiber and has antioxidants that prevent heart disease and cancer. They are rich in Vitamin B6 and Vitamin D which are critical for immune system and overall health. It is low in calories and high in Vitamin A (five times the daily required levels of 900 mg), rich in fiber and a reasonable source of protein (roughly 2grams / sweet potato), this is surely a superfood.

One might think that due to their sweet taste and carbohydrate-rich status, they are not good for diabetics, but the high Vitamin A level actually exerts a positive effect on insulin and blood sugar levels. High homocysteine levels are associated with an increased risk of heart attack and stroke. Vitamin B6 present in sweet potatoes convert homocysteine into other benign molecules.

Tamarind

It is a good source of iron, which balances red blood cell counts in the body. It is full of antioxidants and has surprising health benefits. Studies have shown that some of the antioxidants in tamarind may be an important source of cancer-preventive antioxidants. It is also a good source of minerals like iron, selenium, potassium and copper. Tamarind extract works well in curries and gravies as a replacement for tomato puree. It is also used in sambhar, rasam, chutney and other south Indian preparations.

Tomatoes

Recent studies have revealed that tomatoes are capable of fighting stomach cancer and the fruits' extracts can inhibit growth of malignant cells. Studies have revealed that treatment with whole tomato extracts affected key processes within cells hindering their migration ability, arresting cell cycle through modulation of retinoblastoma family proteins and specific cell cycle inhibitors, and ultimately inducing cancer cell death through apoptosis.

Taro root

Vitamins A and C and various other phenolic antioxidants present in this root boost immune system.

Wheatgrass

It is a concentrated source of nutrients and has high levels of Vitamin A, C and E. It is also rich in iron, calcium, magnesium and amino acids. It can be used to boost immune system. It helps in flushing out toxins.

Fantastic fruits

Avocados

This may hold the key to elixir of life. The fruit can help fight- off diseases including cancer, by tackling dangerous molecules.

Dates

It is rich in iron and help to regulate metabolism, body temperature and immunity. Dates are a significant source of minerals, which strengthen bones and fend off osteoporosis.

Guava

National Institute of Nutrition, Hyderabad, conducted epidemiological research in 2010 to find out the antioxidant levels in 14 commonly available fresh fruits and 10 dried fruits, like guavas, apples, grapes, Indian plums, custard-apples, mangoes, pomegranates, walnuts and cashew nuts. The surprise winner was guava.

A 100 gram medium-sized guava contains around 260 mg Vitamin C (the recommended intake is 75-90 mg per day) and 8.5 gram of dietary fiber (the recommended intake is 25-30 gram per day). It is also rich in carotenoids and potassium. Antioxidant property of guava was found to be 496 mg / 100 gram, the highest among all the tested fruits.

Pink guavas are rich in lycopene and Vitamin A; the latter plays an important role in maintaining healthy skin and mucous membranes. Consumption of foods naturally rich in Vitamin A is known to protect against lung and mouth cancers.

Kiwi

It has vitamin E, which protects and guards against collagen damage caused by UV rays.

Musk melon

It contains high doses of Vitamin A and beta carotene.

Oranges

They are a rich source of beta-cryptoxanthin, which reduces one's risk of developing lung cancer.

Pomegranate

Scientists are describing it as the, 'Swiss Army Knife,' of natural pharmaceuticals because it can do so many things- from improving heart health, lowering blood pressure, treating inflammation, reducing the risk of cancers to tackling sexual dysfunction.

Papaya extract

Researchers from University of Florida have claimed that papaya leaf extract and its tea have dramatic cancer-fighting properties against a broad range of tumours, backing a belief held in a number of folk traditions. Researchers used an extract made from dried papaya leaves, and the effects were stronger when cells received larger-doses of papaya leaf tea. Scientists showed that papaya leaf extract boosts production of key signaling molecules called Th1-type cytokines, which help regulate immune system. This could lead to therapeutic treatments that use immune system to fight cancers.

Pineapple

It is a storehouse of nutrients having Vitamin C and minerals like potassium, copper, manganese, calcium, magnesium, beta-carotene, thiamin, folate as well as soluble and insoluble fiber.

The health benefits are given below:

a)   Arthritis management- It reduces inflammation of joints and muscles, particularly those associated with arthritis;

b)   Tissue and cellular health- Vitamin C in fruit helps in maintaining tissues and walls of the blood vessels and helps in cellular health;

c)   Immune system- A single serving of the fruit has more than 130% of the daily requirement of Vitamin C for human beings, making it one of the richest and most delicious sources of ascorbic acid. Vitamin C is mainly associated with reducing illnesses and boosting immune system by stimulating the activities of white blood cells which act as antioxidants to defend against harmful effects of free radicals;

d)   Bone health- Large amount of manganese which is a trace element present in the fruit (a single serving can deliver more than 70% of the daily requirements) strengthens bones, as well as assist their growth and repairs them; and

e)   Cancer prevention- Apart from Vitamin C the fruit also is rich in other antioxidants like Vitamin A, beta-carotene, bromelain, various flavonoid compounds and high levels of manganese which is an extremely potent free radical scavenger. Pineapple is effective in preventing cancers of mouth, throat and breast.

Rasberries

It has antioxidants, which help to reduce inflammation and heal damaged cells.

Raisins

It is packed with iron, which boosts immune system and helps the body to manufacture amino acids.

Red and purple fruits

Fruits like cherries, strawberries, blackberries, blueberries, and rasberries contain anthocyanins. These powerful flavonoids help inhibit production of certain inflammatory chemicals. These compounds also contribute to the health of connective tissue and defuse attack from free radicals.

Star fruit

It is a good source of B-complex vitamins and pyridoxine, which boost metabolism.

Watermelon

It contains lycopene, which improves heart health, bone health and prevents prostate cancer.

Healing herbs

Aloe Vera

Aloe Vera juice helps to improve immune system and helps in prevention as well as fighting diseases like cancer. It stimulates tissue regeneration and brings great results for the skin. It also aids in absorption of nutrients and neutralizes toxic and bad elements. It is beneficial for diabetic patients. If used over a period of time, it helps in overall body benefits as well as acts as an age defying element.

Take 30 ml of Aloe Vera juice diluted with water early morning for maximum benefit.

Ajwain (Trachyspermum Ammi)

It is rich in fiber, minerals, vitamins and antioxidants.

Amalaki / amla (Indian Gooseberry)

It is the richest source of antioxidants and helps to build immune system. It has unique antioxidant effects and helps to rid off free-radicals. Amalaki fruit extract is available in tablet form.

As mentioned in the book, *Healing Through Natural Foods,* by H K Bakhru, repeated lab tests on Indian gooseberry in Coonoor, Tamil Nadu, have shown that every 100 gram of this fresh fruit provides 470-680 mg. of Vitamin C. Vitamin C offers protection against asthma, bronchitis, cataract, arrhythmia (irregular heartbeat), angina (chest pain due to the hardening of coronary arteries) and cancer of all types. Vitamin C is an important antioxidant which has been shown to regenerate other antioxidants like Vitamin E.

Total antioxidant content of more than 3,100 foods, beverages, spices, herbs and supplements used worldwide, published in the Nutrition Journal ('Antioxidant Food Table', Carisen, et al., 2010), lists Indian gooseberry with an antioxidant score of 261.53millimoles (mmol)/100g. Compare this with the antioxidant score of 9.24 for blueberries. Smokers who need to consume more Vitamin C than non-smokers could do with the extra boost from *amla.*

An ounce of fresh amla juice diluted with water and if required, sweetened with a teaspoon of honey, makes for an excellent tonic in the morning, especially when it's in season. It can be preserved in turmeric-infused brine or sun-dried, and its superfood properties can be enjoyed throughout the year.

Cardamom

It is a good source of potassium, which helps control heart rate and blood pressure. It also contains riboflavin, niacin and Vitamin C, which strengthen immune system.

Cinnamon and Honey

It is claimed that this combination can practically cure everything.
Benefits of cinnamon: It reduces inflammation and can protect against cancer.
It lowers cholesterol level and is also good for diabetic patients.

Benefits of honey: It contains nutraceuticals, which expel free radicals from the body, thereby boosting immunity.
It takes approximately 2 million flowers for a bee to make one pound of honey. It is the only food that doesn't spoil.

Honey cinnamon combination can reduce the risk of heart disease.

Clove

It acts as an anti-inflammatory and antioxidant substance. It is an excellent source of manganese, calcium and magnesium.

Garlic

Garlic contains a little bit of almost everything a human body needs.
Dosage: 2 grams of raw garlic, which is about 3 medium sized cloves per day.

Giloy

It is a powerhouse of antioxidants. It helps to fight free radicals and keep cells healthy. It eliminates toxins, purifies the blood, and fights bacteria that cause diseases. It is also a good immune-modulator and helps to strengthen immune system.
Take two to three leaves of giloy, crush them, and mix with water-drink the juice thus extracted, once a day.

Ginger

6- Gingerol, a substance found in raw ginger has powerful anti-cancer and anti- inflammatory properties. It has potent active ingredients which address a spectrum of health disorders. Gingerols are found to be effective in preventing some types of cancers. A research paper published in the journal, Cancer Prevention Research, found that ginger could cut the risk of colon cancer. It is also found to be effective in treating ovarian cancer. It boosts immune system and helps in the elimination of toxins from the body.

Ginseng

Medicinal properties of this herb are known for more than 5000 years. It is a widely used drug all over the world. It is mainly grown in Korea, Japan and China. Ginseng extract is found to provide more potent protection than ginseng tea. Panax Ginseng, also called as Chinese Ginseng is the main representative of the ginseng family. Ginseng is believed to prevent cancer.

Green Tea

It is the freshest and least processed form of tea. Tea leaves are steamed to soften them, then rolled and dried. It contains antioxidants, powerful polyphenols and has demonstrated anticancer properties. In terms of antioxidant protection is concerned, green tea contains as much Vitamin-C as one glass of orange juice. Drinking at least one cup of green tea three times a day is recommended.
Elderly adults who regularly drink green tea may stay more agile and independent than their peers over time, according to a Japanese study that covered thousands of people. Antioxidants present in green tea may help to ward off cell damage that can lead to disease.

A spoon of lemon or citrus juice with green tea can help absorb a whopping 80 percent of green tea's cancer fighting antioxidants.

Neem

It may stop HIV from multiplying.

Oregano

This herb used in pizza can be used to treat prostate cancer.

Pepper (white)

It helps in burning fats accumulated in the body, resulting in weight loss.

Saffron

A new study has found that saffron, commonly used as a spice to add flavor and colour to food, provides an anti-cancer protective effect by promoting cell death, inhibiting proliferation of cancerous cells, and blocking inflammation.

Safranal, a volatile oil in saffron, has a cytotoxic effect on cancer cells, and has antidepressant properties.

Spirulina

It is blue - green algae that live in the bodies of warm, fresh water. It is a rich source of nutrition, taken as a dietary supplement in the form of powder, tablet or juice. It contains 70% protein, vitamin A and C, and is a powerful cleanser and energy booster.

Researchers in India have found that spirulina, reversed a precancerous condition of the mouth called oral leukoplakia in 45 percent of patients taking this supplement over a one year period.

Tulsi (Basil)

It is rich in antioxidants.

Turmeric

It has anti-bacterial, anti-carcinogenic, and anti-inflammatory properties.

Turmeric juice prevents metastatis- spread of cancer in new areas of human body.

To enhance the absorption of turmeric in the body, pair it with black pepper.

Quinoa

It can provide the protein requirements for the vegetarians.

Cancer cure is in the kitchen

It has been found that turmeric, garlic, ginger, saffron and capsicum, used to spice up Indian curries, have cancer-fighting qualities. While research on curcumin (a turmeric derivative) is in the human trial stage, animal trials have shown good results as per the scientists at the Indian Science Congress. In most US pharmacies, curcumin is available in tablet form.

Food pairings

Food pairings play more important role. Compatible pairing ensures better absorption and better health benefits. Seven favourable matches are given below:

a) *Green tea and lemon* – Green tea is rich in powerful antioxidants like catechins. Scientists say the Vitamin C in citrus fruits can improve catechin absorption.

b) *Broccoli and tomatoes-* Broccoli and tomatoes both have cancer-fighting agents, but research shows eating them together offers more protection. Both are effective at slowing the growth of cancerous prostate tumours than eating either vegetable alone. Eat at least one and a half-cups of broccoli and two and a half cups of fresh tomato.

c) *Red bell peppers and black beans-* This combination will help in the absorption of more immune boosting iron. Iron in beans exists in a form called non-heme, iron that's harder for the body to absorb than the one found in red meat. However, adding a dose of Vitamin C rich food like red peppers converts the iron into a type that's easier for the body to use and boost immunity.

d) *Avocado and green salad-* This combination helps in the absorption of more skin protecting plant compounds called carotenoids from the vegetable salad by adding a little avocado. Carotenoids reduce free radical damage and protect skin from the harmful effects of UV rays. A recent study showed people who ate avocado in their salad of lettuce, spinach and carrots absorbed up to 15 times more carotenoids than those who didn't eat their salads with avocados. Studies show carotenoids require some fat to be optimally absorbed by the body, which means avocados, which contain solid stores of healthful monounsaturated fat, can make a perfect pairing.

e) *Apricots and almonds*- This power pair helps to prevent LDL (bad) cholesterol from oxidizing, a process that happens whenever LDL reacts with free radicals. Oxidized LDL is harmful because it encourages dangerous plaque build-up in arteries. However, in a recent study, researchers have found that phytochemicals in almonds reduced LDL oxidation, when paired with antioxidant Vitamins E and C, both of which are found abundantly in apricots.

f) *Garlic and onions*- These aromatic veggies both contain a number of organosulfur compounds, which are heart healthy plant chemicals that help keep arteries flexible and free of plaque. Some of these compounds have been studied for their power to detoxify carcinogens (cancer-causing substances) in the body. Eating both at the same time increases the chances of getting more of these healthy compounds. Cooked together, they make a delicious base for gravies, curries, soups and sauces or simply stir fry in a mix of olive oil, garlic and onions.

g) *Cinnamon and whole grain toast*- Sprinkling cinnamon may help in keeping blood sugar at a healthier level and in reducing the rise in blood sugar levels after meals. Experts say it is possible to extract more protective compounds when cinnamon is fresh.

Nutritious seeds, oils and nuts

Seeds

Black sesame seeds

It contains saponin enzyme which protects against cervical and breast cancer.

Dill (Suwa / Anethum Graveolens)

It is a rich source of calcium and helps in maintaining bone density. It prevents loss of bone marrow.

Fenugreek

While all spices and condiments have unique properties, fenugreek (methi) seeds seem to contain some very special therapeutic benefits as well. They are good for diabetics, weight watchers, have cholesterol lowering and cancer prevention properties. In addition, they have been reported to have anti-ulcer, anti-fertility, anti-microbial, anti-parasitic properties and protective effects in liver damage.

A decoction of fenugreek seeds is known to reduce glucose levels in blood and urine, and help relieve symptoms of diabetes.

For better effects, powdered seeds can be taken as a drink in water or in buttermilk 15 minutes before a meal.

Photochemical (saponins) and a branched-chain amino acid in fenugreek have also been claimed to aid in glucose, lipid metabolism and cancer protection. Among spices, fenugreek seeds have been known to have high flavonoid content, a type of Photochemical (plant chemical).

A study reported that saponins (particularly, diosgenin and protodioscin) have been known to have cancer preventive properties.

Germinated fenugreek seeds are considered to be more beneficial than dried seeds due to the increased presence of flavonoids and polyphenols.

Fenugreek seeds should not be consumed raw; they are better taken soaked or powdered.

Flax seeds

It is a wonder food since it is rich in Omega-3 fatty acids. A new study has claimed eating a diet rich in flaxseeds can help cut the risk of dying from breast cancer later in life by 40%.

Researchers at the German Cancer Research Centre in Heidelberg found that foods including seeds, vegetables and wheat contain special plant compounds, called phytoestrogens, which kill cancer cells and prevent secondary tumours.

Most important phytoestrogens are found abundantly in flaxseeds. Once in the body, these phytoestrogens attach to female sex hormone oestrogen and are thought to help protect against cancer.

Mustard seeds

Seeds contain glucosinolate which help combat various types of cancers.

Pumpkin seeds

It is rich in zinc and magnesium.

Soya bean

It is packed with anti-cancer properties. It contains active compounds called as isoflavones which is considered as nature's anticancer medication.

It can be consumed through soy milk, tofu, miso (a type of soya paste) etc.

Sunflower seeds

It is a good source of selenium, a trace mineral that prevents cancer.

Watermelon seeds

It acts as diuretics and removes water retention.

Suggestion:

Roast 100 grams each of the above seeds and eat a spoonful with breakfast every morning.

Healthy oils

Olive oil

It is one of the safest and healthiest oils to use. It is known to reduce the risk of cancer amongst other diseases. Antioxidants present in olive oil help fight against free radicals that have cancer inducing properties. It also contains Vitamin E and helps in lowering body's cholesterol levels. Diet enriched with olive oil can increase its protective effect on bones. It may prevent osteoporosis and risk of fracture.

Mustard oil

It has glucosinolate, which is anti-cancer. It stops the formation of tumours. It should be combined with other cooking oils to reduce the erucic acid content.

Rice bran oil

It is relatively new oil extracted from rice bran. It has several benefits like Vitamin E, which is an anti-oxidant, and syalene, which is good for skin. It also has mono-unsaturated fatty acids and cholesterol lowering properties. It is ideal for deep frying.

Sunflower oil

It is rich in PUFA, particularly, linoleic acid that lowers the levels of both good and bad cholesterol. This oil needs to be combined and used with other oils, such as red palm oil that are lower in linoleic acid content.

Coconut oil

It is known as 'no cholesterol' oil. It is one of the safest oils. It is to be used in combination with other oils like sunflower oil. Angelina Jolie takes it as part for her breakfast. Indian Ayurveda talks about its healing properties. It is a healthier substitute to refined cooking oils and is a time tested immunity booster. Recent researches have proved that virgin coconut oil is beneficial in increasing HDL or good cholesterol, which helps in preventing coronary heart diseases. Capric acid in the oil stimulates thyroid gland, speeds up metabolism and lowers resting heart rate.

Fat in coconut oil helps to lose weight by increasing metabolism. It is easily absorbed and digested in the body and goes straight into the liver and thereby aiding metabolism.

Ancient ayurvedic practice of oil pulling whitens the teeth by reducing plaque and improving gum health. It is done by swishing three spoonfuls of virgin coconut oil in the mouth every day for about 20 minutes before rinsing. Since mouth is the doorway to the body system, the oil pulling prevents the body from a lot of bacterial and fungal infections.

Soya Bean oil

It is quite low in saturated fat content and is free of cholesterol. It is known to improve immunity and control diabetes.

Ghee (Clarified butter)

Researchers have discovered that ghee is rich in antioxidants and fats in ghee aid absorption of fat-soluble vitamins and minerals from other foods, strengthening immune system. In his book *The 150 healthiest foods on Earth*, Jonny Bowden has written that ghee contains butyric acid, a fatty acid that has antiviral and anti-cancer properties and that raises the level of anti-viral chemical interferon in the body. Ghee is a source of beta-carotene and vitamins A, D, E, and K. Vitamin A, which is absent in other edible oils is naturally present in ghee.

Ghee contains an essential fatty acid called linoleic acid. Studies have shown that linoleic acid is a potent antioxidant. It was found that linoleic acid targeted mitochondria in cancer cells, disrupting their function and eventually killing them, thereby proving that it improved the cells' oxidant status.

It is advised to make ghee at home by bringing unsalted butter to a simmer and skimming out all the milk solids in the end. This process may take about 15 minutes. Ghee prepared this way is free of adulterants and will remain good at room temperature indefinitely without turning rancid.

Overall fat consumption per person must be restricted to 10-15 grams / day, so roughly 2 tsp of melted ghee per day. Ghee has 25% more medium and short-chain fats than butter, and is therefore healthier than butter.

Nuts

Almonds

It is packed with minerals such as calcium and phosphorous that can contribute to strong bones and dental health. With its generous supply of vitamin E, dietary fiber, and antioxidants, almonds have been found to have cancer-preventive effects, especially on colon cancer. Recent studies have also linked the lowering of prostate cancer risk with the boron content in almonds.

A daily helping of a handful of almonds helps in lowering LDL Cholesterol (bad cholesterol that tend to increase fat accumulation in the body), thus improving cholesterol profile and reducing the risk of heart attacks.

Nutmug

It has strong antioxidants and prevents formation of free radicals in the body.

Power of nuts

Table 5- One serving of nuts (28 gms. of nuts) has the nutrition value given below:

Nut	Calories	Total fat (gms)	Protein (gms)	Carbs (gms)	Fiber (gms	Vita. E (% of RDI)	Magnesium (% of RDI)
Almond	161	14	6	6	3.5	37	19
Pistachios	156	12.5	6	8	3	3	8
Walnut	182	18	4	4	2	1	11
Cashew	155	12	5	9	1	1	20
Peanut	176	17	4	5	3	21	11

Superfoods

Superfoods are foods rich in antioxidants such as phytochemicals-substances occurring naturally in plants that are responsible for their colour, taste, smell and texture- and are supposed to deliver remarkable health benefits. In short, they are nutrient-dense foods, providing more nutrients per calorie than most other foods.

Coconut

Coconut was long vilified for its high saturated fat content, but experts say it has many benefits. Every part and product of coconut, be it the water, the white flesh or oil, is loaded with nutrients. Coconut oil, in particular, is considered heart-friendly and good for weight loss because it speeds up metabolism. Coconut increases body temperature and therefore increases metabolism. It actually aids in weight loss rather than impeding it, as is popularly believed. Coconut water is low in sugars and carbohydrates and high in electrolyte potassium. It stops urinary tract infection, kidney stones and various other health problems.

Guava

It has emerged as the king of fruits, elbowing apples and grapes off the ideal diet chart. A recent study has reported
that guavas have the highest concentration of anti-oxidants among Indian fruits. A 100 gram portion of guava contains around 500 milligrams of anti-oxidants, while apples were found to have only a quarter of the anti-oxidants that guavas have.

Gooseberry (Amla)

It contains 445 mg / 100 gm Vitamin C, 20 times more than in orange. Its free radical absorbing capacity is believed to be higher than that of the superfoods-blueberries and strawberries. Ayurveda recommends it for its rejuvenation powers and it inhibits aging process.

Pumpkin

It contains one of the richest supplies of carotenoids (anti-cancer agents). It has beta carotene which reduces cancer of the colon, bladder and the risk of lung cancer in smokers. Pumpkins are also the only vegetarian source of vitamin B12.

Custard apple

This is another kind of apple that can keep the doctor away. It has anti-oxidant levels of 202 mg, almost twice the amount that apple (123 mg) has. It also has vitamins B and C, potassium, iron, calcium and manganese. Vitamin C is a powerful anti-oxidant that mops up free radicals. It improves immunity and boosts haemoglobin level.

Coriander

Coriander leaves are packed with phytonutrients – chemicals with health protecting properties like immunity building, and lowering blood pressure. It has powerful anti-oxidants and fights toxicity caused due to smoking, chemotherapy and pollution.

Unpolished rice

It contains antioxidants; all trace minerals, and several B vitamins. It helps in controlling obesity, diabetes and lowers cholesterol.

Millets

Sorghum (jowar), pearl millet (bajra) and finger millet (ragi) are called millets. Barley and amaranth (rajgira) also come under the family of millets.
- *Ragi:* Calcium content is nearly 350 mg for 100 gm.
- *Barley:* It contains eight essential amino acids and is a rich source of magnesium, potassium, selenium, and phosphorous.
- *Jowar:* Contains tannins and anthocyanins and has been clinically shown to reduce risk of certain type of cancers in humans. It has a thick bran layer, which has many cancer fighting antioxidants, which eliminates free radicals from the body.
- *Rajgira:* It has more than 20% of the recommended daily allowance of calcium, iron and magnesium.

Some more beneficial food items

Beetal leaves

Eating beetal leaves may help fight cancer.

It is beneficial to patients suffering from chronic 'Myeloid Leukaemia.'- the most common form of leukaemia in India, in which the bone marrow makes too many white blood cells and the body refuses to respond to drugs.

Black rice

It is the richest source of antioxidants.

It has excellent cancer fighting properties.

It takes longer time to cook. Soak it overnight or soak much before cooking.

Bran of brown rice

It contains phenols such as tricin, ferulic acid, and caffeic acid, which inhibit proliferation of colon and breast cancer cells.

Cottage cheese

It contains vitamin D and calcium.

Dark chocolates

It contains antioxidants nearly 8 times found in strawberries and flavonoid that help reduce blood pressure.

Gram flour (Besan)

It has healthy unsaturated fats, which help in the reduction in cholesterol levels in the body.

Jaggery

It helps to regulate blood pressure and is very beneficial for anaemics as it is rich in iron.

Moong beans

It balances the bacteria within the digestive tract.
It helps with nutrient absorption and boosts immune system

Yoghurt

It is an excellent source of good-for-the-gut bacteria.
It should ideally be consumed daily.

Savouring Sattu

Sattu is grounded roasted black gram or chana. It is rich in protein, carbohydrates, minerals, vitamins and fiber.

Mix about half a cup of sattu flour with wheat flour to supercharge the rotis. It has high levels of iron, magnesium and manganese.

Avoid eating sattu at night. Sattu drink shall be thin in consistency so that it is easy to digest. Avoid drinking it with milk and consume on empty stomach for best results.

Macrobiotic diet: Yin and Yang approach to healthy eating

Macrobiotic way of eating essentially draws from the Vedic approach to health and healing. This diet is believed to increase energy, resistance to illness and allows one to live a full life in balance.

It is based on the Chinese philosophy of the two opposing yet complementary forces- Yin and Yong.

Yin is the female force, representing darkness, cold and tranquility. Yang is masculine and represents light, heat and aggression. According to macrobiotic philosophy, food also contains Yin and Yang qualities.

Yin and Yong classification is not related to nutrient content but based on the following parameters- the food's colour, pH value, shape, size, taste, temperature, texture, water content, weight, the region and the season in which it is grown and how it is prepared and eaten.

Table 6- Yin, yang and balanced food

Yin	Yang	Balanced
Sugar	Red meat	Whole grains
Tea	Poultry	Cereals and millets
Alcohol	Fish	Fresh fruits
Coffee	Eggs	Brown rice
Milk	Hard cheese	Whole wheat
Cream	Salt	Vegetables and pulses

Macrobiotic diet is composed of whole grains (50-60 percent of each meal), vegetables (25-30 percent of each meal), pulses in the form of legumes (including soyabean), peas and lentils (5-10 percent of daily meals). Nuts and seeds (small amount as snacks), miso (fermented soyabean) soup, herbal teas and small amounts of white meat, seafood, poultry once or twice a week, make up the diet.

A macrobiotic diet lays emphasis on plant food. It is low in calories and saturated fats, and rich in complex carbohydrates. This makes it useful for reducing the risk of obesity, cancer, high cholesterol, high blood pressure and gastrointestinal complaints including constipation. It has shown to be beneficial in cancer prevention particularly prostate cancer and in reducing the risk of colon cancer by 25 percent.

The diet, however, lacks certain vitamins and minerals, and supplements are often required. Strict adherence to the diet may result in the deficiencies of protein, Vitamin B 12, Vitamin D and minerals like zinc, calcium and iron. Macrobiotic food needs to be customized by a qualified nutritionist.

Alkaline diet

Alkaline diet was proposed in 1930's as a natural cancer treatment for almost any cancer. This treatment approach is not well known because it is considered alternative or experimental or even dangerous by the medical and scientific fraternity and hence has been referenced mainly in obscure publications outside the mainstream press.

Before we talk about pH value it is necessary to understand what this pH value signifies. A pH value between 1 and 6.9 is considered acidic, while one from 7.1 to 14 is considered alkaline. Our body is mostly alkaline and its pH level stands at 7.45, making it alkaline.

The principle of pH therapy is very simple. Metabolism of cancer cells has a very narrow tolerance for cellular proliferation (mitosis), which is between 6.5 and 7.5. Hence, it is possible to interfere with cancer cell metabolism by either lowering or raising internal cell pH, and by doing this theoretically it is possible to stop cancer progression.

While lowering cancer cell pH (increasing acidity) is effective against cancer cell mitosis in the lab, increasing acid levels in the live body of a cancer patient puts stress on normal cells, thereby causing a lot of pain. Hence the proposed alkaline therapy is a 'high pH therapy' and has been developed to normalize intracellular pH of the cancer patient's body through elimination of latent acidosis, while increasing the pH of cancer cells to a range above 7.5. According to published research, it is at that pH they revert to a normal cellular apoptosis cycle (programmed cell death).

Alkaline diet, which is primarily plant- based avoids dairy, sugar, wheat and other high-gluten grains as well as an excess consumption of fruits, while emphasizing on fresh vegetables, coconut water and vegetable juices along with cruciferous vegetables and greens. This diet changes the body's intracellular pH to come close to the ideal blood pH of 7.3 / 7.41- a key metabolic accomplishment on the path to longevity.

An alkaline diet based on vegetables and fruits create a less than optimal environment for cancer proliferation, while at the same time strengthens immune system function and supports healthy cells in the body through improved nutrition.

Second step is to use some nutritional mechanism to move internal cancer cell pH from the optimal mitosis range of pH 6.5 to 7.5, to above 8, which shortens the life of the cancer cell. As described by the proponents, alkaline therapy neutralizes acid waste of the cancer which causes so much pain, interferes with anaerobic fermentation of glucose that starts the self-feeding acidic cancer wasting cycle called 'cachexia' and in time, can induce remission. If this theory of alkaline therapy holds true, it should be possible to address cancer without chemotherapy, radiation or surgery and use alkaline therapy as a primary cancer treatment.

However, alkaline therapy outcomes have yet to be documented in a systematic way, such that the medical community could reliably understand the positive impact of the therapy on cancer treatment.

Alkaline therapy could be used in a supporting role to conventional treatment, which will only improve the long-term outcome for cancer patients.

The long life blessing- Longevity Nutrition

Advances in medical science and enhanced nutrition's have helped to increase overall life expectancy of most populations across the globe by a couple of decades. Current life expectancy in India, for example is 66.08 years for men and 68.33 years for women, up by an incredible 50% on an average since the 1960s, according to the US Central Intelligence Agency's (CIA), The World Facebook, 2012.

Contrary to popular belief, genetics play a relatively minor role in longevity. Our life style, in terms of food choices, exercise habits and positive outlook are more relevant.

How long we live depends on how we choose to live. Longevity Nutrition focuses on calorie restriction with optimum nutrition value. This approach minimizes the conditions associated with ageing, such as inflammation of joints, falling memory, poor eyesight, and accumulation of free radicals and toxins in the body.

The focus foods

Omega- 3 fatty acids which are found in flaxseeds, almonds and oily fish can suppress anything from cardiovascular diseases, cancer, and osteoporosis to auto immune disorders.

Vitamin E- Promotes longevity by detoxifying liver and as an antioxidant and protects against oxidative stress.

Vitamin C- It is indispensable to longevity. An adequate intake of this vitamin could increase life expectancy by at least six years.

Folic acid- It is crucial for longevity as it promotes vital functions of cell growth and division. It prevents cancer and mental deterioration associated with ageing. All leafy green vegetables, broccoli etc are good sources of folic acid.

Vitamin K- It promotes longevity in many ways. It controls blood clotting and prevents kidney calcification, cardiovascular diseases and cancer.

Leafy greens are the richest sources of Vitamin K. One cup or 200 grams of spinach provides more than 10 times the recommended daily dietary intake. Parsley, basil, broccoli, turnips and asparagus are good sources of vitamin K.

Studies have shown that among all the minerals required by the body, magnesium is especially important for longevity because of its role in maintaining muscle and nervous systems healthy, keeping heart rhythm steady and bones strong. Spinach, beans, nuts, millets like bajra, jowar and barley are good sources of magnesium.

Other essential elements for longevity are phosphorous for bone health, selenium which acts as an antioxidant and zinc for improving immunity.

You are what you eat

By making right lifestyle and dietary choices it may actually be possible to reduce the risk of disease and perhaps even stop cancer in its tracks. Formula for a cancer protective diet is to eat right, increase fiber intake, go veggie, choose the right fats, cook right, drink plenty of water and include immune system boosters.

a) ***Prefer a plant based diet-*** A predominantly plant based diet helps prevent or fight cancer. Vegetables, fruits, nuts, grains and beans are all plant based foods. Plants are low in fat, contain fiber and are rich in cancer-fighting nutrients. All these three elements boost immune system which in turn helps to fight cancer. Reduce the amount of processed foods. A meal should consist of at least two-thirds of whole grains, vegetables, beans or fruit. Opt for organic food free of pesticides which are also suspected to be carcinogenic.

b) *Increase intake of fiber-* Eating plant-based foods increases the intake of fiber which helps to keep digestive system clean and healthy. Fruits, vegetables and whole grains are rich in fiber. Fiber content in natural and unprocessed foods is higher.

c) *Prefer a vegetarian diet-* Vegetarians have been shown to have almost 50 percent lesser chances of developing cancer than who eat meat. This is probably because meat lacks fiber and certain nutrients which protect against cancer. Meat also contains fat, especially high levels of saturated fat which has been linked to higher rates of cancer. How the meat is cooked also decides if it can result in formation of compounds which can increase the risk of cancer. It is advisable to reduce the amount of animal based products being consumed. Especially, cut down consumption of red meat, which is high in saturated fats. Add plant-based foods to a meat meal. Prefer a portion of fresh fish or chicken; avoid processed meats like salami, hotdogs or sausages. Make healthier meat and protein choices.

d) *Make right fat choices-* All fats are not bad. Red meat, whole dairy products and eggs are high in saturated fats while partially hydrogenated oils are rich in trans- fats and should be avoided. Unsaturated fats come from plant sources and are protective. These include olive oil, canola oil, nuts and avocados. Omega-3 fatty acids help fight inflammation and are good for brain and heart health. Salmon, tuna and flaxseeds are good sources.

e) *Opt for cancer fighting foods-* Immune system helps to protect the body from infection as well as cancer. Include fruits and vegetables which are rich in antioxidants. The best sources of antioxidants include beta- carotene, vitamin C, vitamin E, and selenium. More colourful the fruits and vegetables the higher the diet is in phytochemical, a potent disease-fighting and immune- boosting nutrient. Garlic, ginger, and curry powder which help add flavor and taste to foods are known to be immune-boosting and help fight cancer; as do turmeric, basil, rosemary, and coriander. Water stimulates immune system. Drink plenty of water; it helps to remove waste and toxins, while delivering nutrients to cells and organs.

A well-balanced diet is the first and probably the most difficult step towards well-being. Improving your diet and nutritional intake can help you live a longer and healthier life. Eat a diet high in foods as whole as possible, with the least amount of processed, adulterated, or sweetened additives. Nutritional supplementation (including vitamins, minerals, herbs, and superfoods) is also important to correct deficiencies.

- From the book-'Longevity-An Alternative Medicine Definitive Guide.'

Experts say fruits should be eaten between meals, not along with lunch or dinner, because they slow down digestion. In fact, fruits are best absorbed on an empty stomach, early morning, as a snack between two meals, or before or after a workout to refuel the body.

Fruits are rich source of vitamins, minerals, natural sugars, enzymes, fibre and antioxidants. In addition to these nutritional values, fruits protect from heart disease, stroke, certain cancers, gastrointestinal issues, high blood pressure, eye disease and chronic diseases.

Cold press juicers extract juice by first crushing and then pressing fruit and vegetables for the highest juice yield. They are said to be healthier than juices made from conventional juicers because of the lack of heating in the grinding process. That helps in keeping the nutrient content higher and they have more enzymes and vitamins even post processing.

Be it gut health or simply to detoxify and clean the system, to reduce water retention or to get the daily intake of fruits, cold pressed juices can help.

Cold pressed juice is absorbed very rapidly by the body and the consumer gets the energy almost instantaneously within a few minutes of drinking it.

References

1. Mint, Mumbai edition dated 9 November, 2010.

2. The Times of India, Mumbai edition dated 16 September, 2011.

3. The Times of India, Mumbai edition dated 30 October, 2011.

4. Mint, Mumbai edition dated 25 September, 2012.

5. Mint, Mumbai edition dated 26 March, 2013.

6. Mumbai Mirror dated 9 September, 2013.

7. Mumbai Mirror dated 17 January, 2017.

8. Ishi Khosla, Indian Express dated 11 March, 2017.

9. Ishi Khosla, Indian Express, Mumbai edition dated 22 April, 2017.

10. The Times of India, Mumbai edition dated 15 May, 2017.

11. 'Lower your cancer risk now' – Dr. Mitchell L Gaynor and Jerry Hickey.

12. http://www.greenmedinfo.com/blog/why-alkaline-approach-can-successfully-treat-cancer

Living in harmony

The Sun is a daily reminder that we too can rise again from the darkness
that we too can shine our own light

Human body is capable of self-healing, self-recuperating and self-regenerating. Everyone is blessed with the capability of living a disease free life in good health. But this boon comes with certain conditions. The conditions are- human beings shall live under natural conditions and, they need to live in harmony with nature. Living in harmony with nature will build health and there may not be any need to treat or cure diseases.

Good health can be maintained by breathing pure air, moderate exercise, consuming natural food, occasional fasting, massaging, Sun bathing, practicing relaxation, meditating and engaging in other holistic practices. It is necessary to adopt a lifestyle that is in sync with nature. Health is not only the absence of disease symptoms but also a state of overall physical, mental, spiritual and emotional well being.

Several scientific studies have revealed that living in harmony with nature can ensure a disease free life. This section explains various methods of harnessing the power of nature to maintain a perfect health in a natural way, without the use of medicines.

This section also reveals how to develop a lifestyle that helps reduce dependence on medication.

Moderate exercise

Several studies have found that 30-45 minutes of daily exercise reduces risk of developing many potentially fatal illnesses including Coronary Heart Disease (CHD). Brisk walking for at least 30 minutes per day is the best possible exercise.

According to research published in The American Journal of Hypertension, 61 to 90 minutes of exercise a week is an effective way to lower systolic blood pressure but exercising more than 90 minutes a week was not seen to have any increased benefit when it came to lowering blood pressure or heart risks associated with it.

Even a little goes a long way

A research conducted by University of Sydney studied health and habits of 63,000 adult respondents. The researchers found a consistent pattern of hitting the gym one or optimally two times a week lowers the risk of dying from illnesses, including cancer and cardiovascular diseases.

It is very encouraging news that being physically active on just one or two occasions per week is associated with a lower risk of death, even among people who do some activity, but don't quite meet recommended exercise levels. However, for optimal health benefits from physical activity, it is always advisable to meet and exceed the physical activity recommendation.

(As reported in Economic Times-ET Panache, dated 24 February, 2017)

Micro workouts

This is about adding sporadic micro-bursts of physical activity to ones daily routine. For instance, the '7 Minute
Workout' app that ranks number one in 127 countries has been documented by over two million people. Micro workouts can be anything from brisk walking, jumping rope, and climbing stairs or, bike riding etc. Short bursts of high-intensity actions are as beneficial as longer, less aggressive routines, like jogging.

Over 60 must exercise once a week

Women over the age of 60 may need to exercise only once a week to improve their strength and endurance, a new study has claimed. Researchers at the University of Alabama at Birmingham monitored 63 women performing combined aerobic exercise training (AET) and resistance exercise training (RET) for 16 weeks.

One group performed AET and RET one time per week, a second group two times per week and the third group three times per week. The study found significant increases in muscular strength, cardiovascular fitness and functional tasks in each group, but there were no significant differences in outcomes among the groups. This study demonstrated that doing as little as one AET and one RET workout each week could provide a lot of benefit for older women's overall quality of life and health. The researchers said that the study went against what most people believed about exercise- that more is better.

Greater frequency, intensity and duration of exercise training have been shown to be beneficial in younger adults. This study suggests that progressive overload that benefits a younger demographic may not necessarily apply to all aspects of health and fitness in women over the age of 60.

(Source: Mumbai Mirror, dated 9 September, 2013)

Oil massage

Ayurveda refers self- massage as 'abhyanga' and credits this with several benefits. Massage involves rubbing and manipulating the muscles, tendons, skin and ligaments with oil. A full body massage offers multiple benefits, both physically and psychologically. The benefits are given below:

a) Increased blood circulation- Associated Bodywork & Massage Professionals state that the massage can increase blood circulation and also can help oxygen and nutrients to reach tissues and organs. A massage may help control blood pressure.

b) Reduced stress, anxiety and depression- A massage reduces stress levels in most people. It also gives other benefits such as better sleep, increased energy levels and less fatigue.

c) Immune system function- A full body massage may increase immune system's function. Massage stimulates lymphatic system which in turn helps immune system to protect the body.

(Caution: Consult physician / oncologist if you have medical conditions such as cancer, fractures, blood clots, rheumatoid arthritis, osteoporosis or pregnant)

Forest bathing

Japanese art of 'forest bathing' is an excellent wellness break. A study conducted across 24 forests in Japan found that when people strolled in a wooded area, their levels of stress hormone 'Cortisol' dropped almost 16% more than when they walked in an urban environment. One of the biggest benefits of being in a forest comes from breathing in stress relieving chemicals called 'Phytoncides' emitted by the trees and the plants. In a forest setting hormones reach a harmonious balance. In this environment all kinds of healing are possible.

(The Times of India, Mumbai edition dated 19 February, 2017)

Exposure to Sun protects from 15 types of cancer

Scientists have discovered that exposure to Sun may protect against some forms of cancer, despite increasing the risk of skin cancer. In a series of studies, lack of sunlight was linked to 15 types of cancer. In one, researchers assessed cancer cases in 100 countries along with ambient ultraviolet radiation rates. More sunlight was 'consistently' tied to reduced rates of many types of cancer including breast, cervical, colon, oesophageal, gastric, lung and two forms of lymphoma. The researchers said Vitamin D, produced by sunlight may reduce the incidence or improve the outcome of cancer.

It is advised to get enough sunlight. Sunbathing everyday for about 15 to 20 minutes is recommended.

(Source: The Times of India)

Staying close to nature can help fight depression

The fact that a refreshing breeze, warm rays of life-giving sunlight and sweet-smelling greenery can work its magic on not just ailing patients but even on healthy people is not new. A few days ago, environmental psychologist Roger Ulrich demonstrated that gazing at a garden can speed up the healing process of patients who have undergone surgery or have infections and other ailments.

Researchers John Zelenski and Elizabeth Nisbet have found that the 'nature relatedness' has a distinct happiness benefit. The psychologists say that the nature plays an extremely significant role when it came to maintaining a positive mental health.

(Source: Business Times dated 7 May, 2017)

Plant and positive energy

Keeping plants inside the house not only adds to the aesthetics but is also useful in many other ways. It brings in a lot of positive energy, adds to the ambience, helps inmates to relax and acts as a natural purifier.

The plants also can help in getting better sleep at night. But there can be an argument against this since plants also give out carbon dioxide in the night as part of the photosynthesis process.

However, it is proven that certain plants use far less oxygen than what is usually perceived. Here are a few plants that can be kept in the bedroom which will help in sleeping well in the night.

Spider plant:

It is said to cleanse the air of cancer-causing chemicals. Plant also absorbs adours and helps to sleep better.

Snake plant:

According to NASA, snake plant is one of the best air filtering house plants. It emits oxygen in the night, and so, is a great choice to be kept in the bedroom.

Jasmine:

It has soothing effect on the body. The plant is said to reduce anxiety levels in a person and brings in a lot of positive energy.

Aloe Vera:

Besides being used for skin creams, these plants can help one to sleep well. The plant emits oxygen in the night. It is easy to grow and maintain.

Lavender:

Everyone likes the scent of this plant. The plant helps to reduce anxiety and stress levels and can help in sound sleep. The researchers have proven that this plant can help babies to slip into deep sleep and can also reduce stress levels in new mothers.

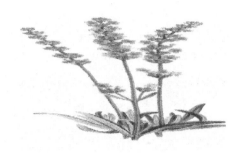

(Source: Bombay Times, dated 19 March, 2017)

Power of deep breathing

Stress management is an important key for improving health and quality of living. Energy levels depend on a great extent on the breath we take. Better we breathe, the more energy we will have. Taking deeper breaths will bring in more oxygen to the body and improve the energy levels.

Good breathing habits help lymphatic system to function properly. Deep breathing cleanses blood, and pumps blood to all parts of the body. This encourages the release of harmful toxins from all parts of the body.

Deep breathing exercises can reduce stress levels. Deep breathing stimulates parasympathetic nervous system which slows down the heart rate, thereby lowering the high blood pressure.

Deep breathing exercises strengthen lung muscles and increase the supply of oxygen to the body. Recent studies report that cancer and many other diseases can only live in an acidic body.

Deep breathing is said to reduce acidity levels of the body, making it more alkaline thereby reducing the risk of cancer.

A good thing about deep breathing is that it can be practiced anywhere and anytime and does not cost anything at all. Even 5 minutes of slow deep conscious breathing once or twice a day can bring in huge health benefits.

Positive thinking

It is observed that, faced with stressful situations in life, positive thinkers cope more effectively than pessimists. Studies find that when optimists encounter a disappointment, they are more likely to focus on things that they can do to resolve the situation. Rather than getting lost in the frustration or things that they can't change, they will devise an alternative plan of action and likely to seek advice and help from others. On the other hand, pessimists will simply assume that the situation is quite out of control and there is nothing they can do to overcome it. Studies have found that optimism helps to improve the immunity system.

Human mind can have a powerful effect on the body's immunity system. Thoughts, attitudes and beliefs powerfully influence the immunity system. In one study, researchers concluded that negative emotions and attitudes weakened the response of the human immunity system to a flu vaccine. In diseases like cancer, it is observed that people who were optimistic responded better to treatment and also lived longer.

Positive thinking impacts the ability to cope up with stress, strengthens body's immune system but also impacts health and overall well being. Mayo Clinic, USA reports a number of health benefits associated with optimism, including reduced risk of death from various life threatening diseases and an increased lifespan.

Positive thinking also makes a person more resilient. Resilience refers to the ability to cope up with problems. Resilient people are able to face a crisis or trauma with strength and resolve. Rather than falling apart and disintegrating, in the face of a crisis, they have the ability and resolve to carry on and meet the situation head on. Eventually such people overcome and overpower adversity. When dealing with a challenge, optimists typically look at what they can do to solve the problem. They marshal their resources and ask others for help.

Experts believe that positive attitude and resilience can be developed and cultivated by the individuals. By nurturing positive feelings, emotions and attitudes one can effectively manage stress levels, reduce depression and a strong will to survive against all odds.

Yoga

Yoga provides psychological relief and also helps patients build mental strength to fight against cancer. There are cases where patients have shown improvement in health when yoga is practiced along with chemotherapy or radiation. Side-effects also can be reduced. Some asanas that could provide relief are-suryanamaskar (a cycle of 12 different postures), ardha-chakrasana, ardha-katichakrasana, ustrasana and shashankasana. Asanas must be learned from a trained teacher.

Harness the power of thoughts

People do not utilize the full potential of their minds. It's like spending an entire lifetime craving something, only to realize too late that it was always with you, a package you didn't care to open. Such is the power of the mind. It holds within it all possibilities that one can imagine. However, you need to unpeel the wrapping and get a singular focus of what you intend to do with that astonishing power, once unleashed.

Life, it seems, does not follow the path of our desires and strategies as much as that of the intentions and beliefs. There are instances of people healing themselves or psyching themselves out of a difficult situation. Diagnosed with leukemia some years ago, Dr, Dyer claimed to have cured himself with the power of his mind.

There are reports of patients given a few weeks to live, going on to outlive their doctors' predictions by several years through the power of positive thinking on their bodies.

Dr. Bruce Lipton, developmental biologist explains the phenomena. He says that with the help of our beliefs, we can manipulate the way cells read our genes and DNA. Mind's function is to create coherence between beliefs and reality. If you believe something, positive or negative, mind creates that reality for you, says Dr. Lipton. Body has reserve cells that will replace or heal anything that our attention is focused on.

And so a negative belief can hurt or kill as much as a positive emotion can heal or revive.

Medical research has shown that two-thirds of all healing is done through Placebo effect- mind and belief of the patient determines response to treatment rather than the actual medicine or surgery.

Interestingly, most people do not realize that mind can only think thoughts we allow it to. Thoughts are powerful that travel within and deep into our subconscious levels and influence our behaviour, but they also travel to the Universe and determine not just the behaviour of others towards us, but also the events that transpire.

If this is the strength of thinking, imagine the power we retain if we can direct our own thoughts and mind. Real challenge lies in unraveling the gift of the mind and then harnessing the force thus unleashed. Being aware of our thoughts and the direction they are taking is an important tool in handling them. One must constantly plant positive thoughts and weed out unwanted, negative stuff. You will soon realize how easy it becomes to do so.

Try this. When upset or depressed, identify the cause and tell your mind to put off thinking about the issue for some time. Meanwhile, indulge in happy thoughts in a disciplined manner, rooting out negativity from your mind. By the time you get to refocus on your problem, your mind will be a happier place, and the issue, less threatening.

Dyer strikes a note of warning, saying that most people in applying the 'Law of Attraction' want and demand things.

However, that's not how it works. He refers to an ancient Chinese philosopher Lao Tzu's insistence on virtue as the touchstone for the Law of Attraction. Tzu's four basic virtues- reverence for all life, natural sincerity, gentleness and supportiveness- are the best way to ensure that our mind bridges the gap between our thoughts and reality, says Dyer.

('It's Your Life- Best of O-zone' by Vinita Dawra Nangia, published in
The Times of India)

Creative visualization

Creative visualization is the technique of using your imagination to create what you want in your life. Imagination is the ability to create an idea or mental picture in your mind. In creative visualization you use your imagination to create a clear image of something you wish to manifest. Then you continue to focus on the idea or picture regularly, giving it positive energy until it becomes objective reality.... In other words, until you actually achieve what you have been visualizing.

Creative visualization is the perfect tool for healing because it goes straight to the source of the problem ... your own mental concepts and images.

Method- Relax into a deep, quiet, meditative state of mind. Begin to picture yourself and affirm to yourself that you are in perfect radiant health; see your problem as completely healed and cured.

There are many different approaches that can be taken on many different levels; you need to find the particular type of affirmations and images that work best for you.

Example- You can imagine the cancerous tumour in the specific part of the body being bombarded with powerful beams of energy thereby completely destroying it. While imagining, affirm mentally, 'The powerful beam of energy is destroying all cancer cells. Day by day, and in every way I am becoming better and better.'

(For more information read 'Creative Visualization' by Shakti Gawain)

Fasting

Metabolic activity of human body creates various types of wastes and toxins. Waste removal is of vital concern, as metabolic wastes are poisonous and must be carried away from the cells by blood and lymphatic system, the 'garbage disposal' of the body. Periodic fasting may facilitate removal of toxins, which choke the cells of the body.

True fasting is done by consuming only water or herbal teas with zero calorific value. Fasting on water causes rapid release of internal and external toxins from the body, where they have been buried in fat for long periods of time.

Incorporating vegetable or fruit juices and green foods is less aggressive than a true, water-only fast and is better tolerated by most people. While water fasting is theoretically the best method of detoxification, it should be done strictly under medical supervision.

Antioxidants and lipotropic nutrients shall be taken preceding a water fast in order to support the kidneys and other eliminative organs; toxins can temporarily reach high concentrations in stool, lymph, blood, urine and breath during fasting.

It is best to do fast over a period of eight days. The fast itself usually lasts for five days. It is recommended to slowly re-introduce healthy food back into the diet, over a period of one week and not to end a fast by eating a meal of rich, fatty food.

Day-1- Eat only fruits, vegetables (raw or cooked), tofu, nuts, seeds and juices. Dilute juices by 50-75% with water. Drink at least eight large glasses of water.

Day-2- Consume only raw or steamed vegetables and fruits. Eliminate tofu, nuts and seeds. Limit portions of meals to decrease the capacity of stomach.

Day-3- Eat only raw vegetables and fruits.

Day-4 to 8 – Eliminate all solid foods. Drink unlimited quantities of warm herbal tea throughout the day. Consume liberal quantity of water, which will dilute and flush lymphatic, circulatory, and urinary systems. Urine must remain diluted so that its toxins do not damage the kidneys.

Take the following supplements to support the organs of detoxification and minimize any temporary problems.

a)   Vitamin-C, 1000mg, three times daily;

b)   Vitamin –B Complex; and

c)   Other supplements as recommended by the nutritionist.

Day-9- On the first day of eating solids, consume only one light meal of steamed or baked vegetables. Eat only one type of vegetable and do not mix. Slowly ease into regular diet.

Day-10- Diet can be supplemented with more varieties of cooked, non-fatty vegetarian food and raw salad.

Day- 11 to 13- Reintroduce in to the diet, easily digestible proteins such as tofu, whole grains such as brown rice, millets, quinoa and amaranth.

Day-14 to 15- It is now time to return to normal health diet.

It is once again strongly advised to seek the advice of the consulting / attending doctor before attempting any of the detox methods.

(Source: 'Longevity: An Alternative Medicine Definitive Guide'
by W Lee Cowden and others)

Fasting once or twice a week could help to live longer

For many people the key question regarding fasting is whether it's good or bad for health. Now, a new study says that skipping meals for a couple of days a week could help a person to live longer.

Researchers at the National Institute on Ageing have found that fasting for one or two days in a week is key to a long life because it can protect brain against Alzheimer's, Parkinson's and other degenerative brain conditions. Chemical messengers in brain are boosted when calorie intake is restricted, say the researchers.

It has long been known that severely restricting calorie intake can increase the lifespan of rats and mice and it has been suggested there could be a similar effect in humans too but the theory is difficult to test.

Now, the researchers have found the positive effects of fasting. Researchers suggest going on intermittent bouts of fasting, in which the person eats hardly anything at all, and then have periods when the person eats as much one wishes.

(Reported in Times of India)

Chakra Balancing

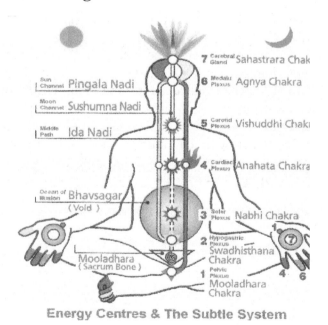

Energy Centres & The Subtle System

Several cultures around the world believe in an energy field, which surrounds everyone and everything. Energy in our body flows through and is regulated by chakras. Chakra comes from Sanskrit word meaning a spinning wheel. They spin, taking in energy, and redirecting it to the body.

Chakras are energy centers. Although most people are familiar with seven chakras of the body, actually there are 114 in the body-comprising of both major and minor chakras. In addition to these 114 chakras, body also has 72,000 'nadis' or energy channels, along which vital energy, or 'prana' moves. When nadis meet at different points in the body, they form a triangle. In fact, this triangle is called as chakras. It is called as a wheel since it symbolizes growth, dynamism and movement, even though it is actually a triangle.

In a healthy body, energy flow is harmonious and all chakras are in perfect equilibrium. In blocked chakras, energy does not flow harmoniously thereby creating imbalance in chakras.

The seven chakras are distributed over the entire body. Each chakra is important for good health and well being of the specific part of the body, which it regulates. Physical manifestation of each chakra is through specific glands / nerves in the endocrine system and the nervous system. An imbalance in chakras is manifested in physical and mental illness.

The seven fundamental chakras are:

1. **Root chakra or Mooladhara-** It is located below the base of the spine, at the perineum, the space between the anal outlet and the genital organ. It controls adrenal gland of the endocrine system. It controls large intestine and rectum, function of kidneys, muscular system, immune system and fat cells.

2. **Spleen chakra or Swadishthana-** Located at lower abdomen, just above the genital organ. It regulates pancreas, liver, kidneys, and the lower abdomen. Dysfunction may lead to blood cancer, diabetes, diseases of spleen and urinary system.

3. **Solar plexus or Manipura chakra-** Located at solar plexus, below diaphragm. It regulates pancreas, spleen, adrenal glands, respiratory system, digestive system, sympathetic nervous system, spleen and liver.

4. **Heart chakra or Anahata-** Located at the chest, just beneath where the rib cage meets. It controls thymus gland, heart and

circulatory system, pulmonary system, immune system, upper back, shoulders and arms.

5. **Throat chakra or Vishuddhi-** Located at the pit of the throat. It controls throat, neck, mouth, teeth, gums, ears, thyroid, and muscles. It regulates thyroid and parathyroid glands of the endocrine system.

6. **Third eye chakra or Ajna chakra -** Located between the eyebrows. It regulates pituitary and pineal glands of the endocrine system. It controls brain, nervous system, eyes, ears, nose and the sinuses. Dysfunction may result in brain tumours, and neurological problems.

7. **Crown chakra or Sahasrara or brahmarandra-** Located at the top of the head or the crown of the head. It controls pineal gland in the brain, central nervous system, cerebrum, top of the spinal cord, brain stem, and nerves.

Ideally the seven chakras are balanced, meaning they have just the right amount of energy flowing through them. In reality, chakras become unbalanced thereby causing diseases.

Chakra balancing is a common form of energy healing. Yoga, Reiki, meditation, visualization, positive affirmations and physical exercises are some of the techniques which can be used to harmonize the chakras. These techniques can be learned under the guidance of an experienced guru.

Creative visualization for chakra balancing is described below:

-    Sit in meditative posture, keeping spine erect;
-    Relax the entire body by any one of the relaxation techniques;
-    Start from the Mooladhara or Root chakra;
-    Visualize the Mooladhara chakra and visualize external positive energy beams energizing this chakra; hold this visualization for thirty seconds;
-    Move on to next chakras- Swadishthana, Manipura till Sahasrara chakra and visualize as before;
-    After energizing all the seven chakras, remain quiet for some time and open your eyes softly.
-    Now all the seven chakras are energized.

Music Therapy / Raga Chikitsa

Music is often linked to mood. A specific song can make one feel happy, sad, energetic, or relaxed. Since music can have such a profound impact on a person's mindset and well-being, music therapy has been studied for use in managing several medical conditions.

All forms of music may have therapeutic effects, although music from one's own culture may be most effective. In Chinese medical theory, five internal organs and meridian systems are believed to have corresponding musical tones, which are used to encourage healing.

There is something called as the 'Mozart Effect,' which make people listening to music, especially classical music to feel better. Studies have shown that soothing classical music is often played in post-anesthesia centers because of its ability to improve comfort and reduce pain. At McGill University in Montreal, neuroscientists have concluded that music activates different parts of the brain, depending on what music is listened to.

Music may also be used to relax and also can be used with guided imagery to produce altered states of consciousness that help uncover hidden emotional responses and stimulate creative insights. Classical music has been found to induce comfort and relaxation.

Once a rarely offered therapy, both the profession and therapeutic intervention have grown substantially in the United States. In US, 30 of 41 National Cancer Institute- designated Comprehensive Cancer Centers offer music therapy for patients.

There is no evidence at present that music therapy can treat cancer as well. Like any other psychological therapy,
some people may find music therapy helpful, while others may not.

However, there is evidence that music therapy can help people relax and can reduce stress and anxiety. Other studies suggest that it may improve quality of life for people living with cancer.

It is not necessary for anyone to have musical ability or experience to benefit from music therapy. Brain and body naturally respond to sound, including rhythm and beat of the music.

Music therapy has been found to be effective under the conditions listed below and there are scientific supporting evidences to prove its effectiveness:

1) *Autism-* People who have autism spectrum disorders often show a heightened interest and response to music. This may aid in teaching of verbal and nonverbal communication skills and in establishing normal developmental processes.

2) *Dementia-* In older adults with Alzheimer's, dementia, and other mental disorders, music therapy has been found to reduce aggressive or agitated behaviour, reduce symptoms of dementia, improve mood, and improve cooperation with daily tasks, such as bathing. Music therapy may also decrease the risk of heart or brain diseases in elderly dementia patients.

3) **Depression-** There is evidence that music therapy may increase responsiveness to anti-depressant medications. In elderly adults with depression, a home-based programme of music therapy may lead to reductions in heart rate, respiratory rate, blood pressure and depressed mood.

4) *Sleep quality-* In older adults, music therapy may result in significantly better sleep quality as well as longer sleep duration, greater sleep efficiency, shorter time needed to fall asleep, and less sleep disturbance

Raga Chikitsa

It means healing through the use of 'raga.' It is the usage of raga for the purpose of healing. Fundamental features of 'raga chikitsa' is the classification of the ragas based on their elemental composition- ether, air, fire, water and earth- and proper use of the elements to balance the nature of the imbalance.

Carnatic music (popular in Southern part of India) is very scientific and there are 72 Melakarta (parent ragas) ragas. These 72 ragas have 7 (SRGMPDN) swaras in Aarohanam (high pitch) and in Avrohanam (low pitch). The music system is created using permutation and combination of swaras and swarasthanas. Innumerable 'Child Ragas' are derived from parent (Melakarta) ragas.

One of the unique features of Indian classical music is the assignment of definite times of the day and night for performing or listening to raga melodies. It is believed that only in this period the raga appears to be at its best.

Seven swaras and their affinity with the chakras

Seven swaras of the ragas are closely associated with a particular chakra of the body both in high pitch and in low pitch. The association is given below:

1. *Sa- (S)* – Mooladhara chakra;
2. *Ri (R)*- Swadishthana chakra;
3. *Ga (G)*- Manipura chakra;
4. *Ma (M)*- Anahata chakra;
5. *Pa (P)*- Vishuddhi chakra;
6. *Da (D)* – Ajna chakra;
7. Ni *(N)* – Sahasrara chakra

Ragas and their effects

Several researches conducted on ragas have revealed a positive correlation between ragas and their therapeutic effects. Some of the therapeutic effects are given below:

Raga	Therapeutic effects
Amrutavarshini	Alleviates diseases related to heart
Ananda Bhairavi	Reduces kidney problems, controls blood pressure
Bhairavi	Reduces anxiety, provides relief to cancer patients
Bahidari	Removes depression and brings joyous feeling
Charukesi	Rejuvenates the mind helping one to age gracefully
Darbari	Effective in easing tension. Composed by Tansen.
Hansadhwani	Gives energy, helpful in treating several diseases
Kalyani	Gives energy and removes tension. Many authentic reports exist about the raga's power to destroy fear.
Kapi	Helps in managing depression and anxiety
Karaharapriya	Curative for heart disease
Kedaram	Gives energy and removes tension
Kolahalam	Removes sorrow and brings in joyous feeling
Madhuvarshini	Good for nervous system.
Maya Malavala Gowla	Counters pollution
Neelambari	Cures insomnia
Ranjani	Cures kidney disease
Rohini	Cures back pain, joint pain etc.

Shivaranjani	Powerful raga for meditation, good for general health
Shankarabharanam	The power of this raga is incredible. Power to shower wealth. Cures mental illness.
Shanmugapriya	Instills courage, energizes the body
Vasantham	Cures paralysis
Vinodhini	Powerful raga. Can bring back life to the dead.
Vishwambari	General wellbeing.

Music therapy in supportive cancer cure

A cancer diagnosis is one of the most feared and serious life events that cause stress in individuals and families. Commonly experienced by cancer patients are also fear of death and disease recurrence, the problems related to long and short term effects of treatment, changes in personal relationships and economic issues. The idea that patients with cancer may benefit from musical expression and musical experiences has been supported by music therapy research. Music therapy not only helps patients to cope up with their negative emotions, it can also be used to benefit patients in a complex way as music is the most fundamental and unique form of art that affects people spiritually, emotionally, socially and physically.

- National Center for Biotechnology information, US National library of medicine.

Caution

Music should not be used as the sole treatment for potentially dangerous medical or psychiatric conditions. Use of music is also not recommended in those cases who do not like music therapy as this may result in agitation or stress. Always, consult the doctor before trying out any new complementary or alternative therapies.

Deal with fear through positive affirmations

'What is courage?

And how to overcome fear?

Courage is not the absence of fear,

but rather the judgment that something else is more

important than fear.

- Ambrose Redmoon

Fear is a pernicious problem that shuts down our life force. Like depression or any other problem that inhibits the flow of positive energy, fear starts a negative cycle that becomes self-reinforcing.

Decreased energy causes decrease in a will which, in turn, reduces our energy even further. But there are ways to reverse this cycle. Here are some tools from the spiritual path.

a) Law of opposites: In theory at least, it is easy to overcome any problem. Simply put out equal or greater energy in the opposite direction. The best way to cancel a negative tendency is to develop its positive counterpart. To overcome fear, develop faith or non-attachment.

Start with small steps. Concentrate first on simply increasing the flow of physical energy. Exercise daily, do some deep breathing. Practice the energisation exercises.

Then apply your increased energy to overcome fear. Think of fear like a wildfire in the brain. Stomp out the small sparks right away before they have time to start a conflagration.

b) Non-attachment: Most fear centers around losing some thing you value. The more you develop non-attachment, the less vulnerable you will be. Every night, before you sleep, give all your possessions and all your desires back to God. Make Him responsible for your wellbeing and security.

Try especially to give Him negative desires, the ones that contract your consciousness and cause you to emphasize your ego or little self. They are the main source of our fears and anxiety.

c) Affirmation: Replace fear thoughts through the use of affirmation. Swami Kriyananda suggests to repeat this:

'I live protected by God's infinite light. So long as I remain in the heart of it, nothing and no one can harm me'

It is followed by this prayer:
'I look to Thee for my strength. Lord, Hold me closely in Thy arms of love. Then whatever happens in my life, I shall accept with joy.'

This affirmation will become a powerful ally to help you drive out fear.

d) Visualization: Fear originates in parts of primitive brain that are pre-verbal. Visualization helps reprogramme reactive processes in these areas. Imagine yourself bathed in a golden light that both protects and strengthens you.

e) Giving love and security: To change thought habits, give to others that which you want for yourself. In this case, give love and security to others. Look for at least two opportunities each day to help allay fear in someone else.

One of the opportunities should be for a friend or loved one. But the other, if possible, should be for a stranger. This practice unleashes the infinite power of the law of karma and the Golden Rule, which advices us to give unto others that which we would like to receive ourselves.

Remember, that God's infinite love and protection already surrounds you. Your job is simply to recognize its presence and let it work its magic.

(Source: Nayaswamis Jyotish and Devi, The speaking tree, The Times of India dated 2 June, 2017)

Heartfulness relaxation technique

When body and mind are deeply relaxed, brain wave pattern actually changes and becomes slower. This deeper, slower level is commonly called as 'alpha level,' while busy waking consciousness is called 'beta level.' Several researchers have reported positive benefits of reaching alpha level.

Alpha level has been found to be a very healthful state of consciousness, because of its relaxing effect on mind and body. And interestingly enough, it has been found to be far more effective than the more active beta level in creating real changes in the so-called objective world, through the use of visualization, which is already explained.

If one can learn to relax deeply and do creative visualization, one will be able to make far more effective changes in life.

Process

- Close your eyes. Breathe calmly and slowly, and relax in comfort.
- Relax your toes... your feet...your ankles. Feel your calves relax.... Thighs... and whole legs. Relax your buttocks and hips....your stomach.... Then your chest area. Let go of all tension in your lower back... then upper back.
- Relax your fingertips, hands, lower arms and upper arms. Relax your shoulders; neck... let them melt away.
- Relax your face, your jaw and your lips. Your eyes are closed very gently and very softly. Allow your mind to relax... Move your attention to your heart and stay there for a little while.
- Slowly bring your attention back to the present moment. Wriggle your toes. Slowly, gently, open your eyes.

Above process may take about 3 to 5 minutes. It can be practiced anywhere and anytime. It is advised to do relaxation exercise before starting meditation which is explained next.

Power of meditation- Author's own experience

Over the past few decades, meditation has acquired universal recognition for its numerous positive benefits. Many methods of meditation are being practiced all over the world, and it is possible that all of them are effective.

I was aware of the benefits of meditation and in the past I tried different types of meditation. I learnt 'Vipasana meditation' and practiced for almost about a year. In this method the practitioner focuses on one's own breathing. I learnt 'transcendental meditation' of revered Mahesh Yogi through a Guru. My Guru gave me a specific mantra to chant during meditation. I practiced this form of meditation for more than two years. I also learnt 'yogic meditation' through a Guru. In this type of meditation, the practitioner visualizes a spinning disc at the center of the eye brow (ajna or third eye chakra) and concentrates and meditates on the spinning disc.

I learnt Reiki and went on to become a Grand Master, completing five levels successfully. I practiced Reiki meditation, which involved focusing and meditating on Reiki symbols. I also learnt self-hypnosis through Master Pradeep Agarwal.

All these meditation techniques gave a feeling of well being and mental peace. But somehow I felt that I did not fully experience all the benefits that were really possible through meditation. Meditation if properly done, for a considerable length of time, will strengthen immune system, reduce blood pressure, bring calmness, enhance the intuitive power and bring in many more benefits. It could be possible that I did not get the maximum benefit since I tried out too many varieties in too little time, hopping from one method to another, without giving enough time to each method to show results.

I felt a great difference when I started practicing Sahaj Marg meditation also called as 'Heartfulness meditation.' This meditation is very simple and there is no need to concentrate on anything. But what makes it unique is the addition of another important aspect known as 'pranahuti' or 'yogic transmission'. This yogic transmission makes this meditation method truly dynamic, and it is the real specialty and uniqueness of Heartfulness method offered by Sahaj Marg.

Presently I practice 'Heartfulness Meditation', which comes from Sahaj Marg System of Raja Yoga. In this yogic practice mind is used as the main tool to be in tune with the heart. In this, the practitioner sits with eyes closed and focuses on 'divine light in the heart. It is very simple and at the same time a very powerful technique. In the evening I practice something called as 'cleaning' which is a more active process, where I focus on removing old impressions and all negativity from the energy body.

Sahaj Marg practice is based on the philosophy of human being having a soul, a body and also a subtle body (energy body), and it is this energy body the practitioner works with and refines during meditation. Sahaj Marg is a way for leading one's life.

About Sahaj Marg:

Shri. Ram Chandra of Fatehgarh is the founder of Sahaj Marg. He rediscovered the ancient and long forgotten spiritual technique of yogic transmission, refined it, and offered it as a sure and simple way to achieve the goal of human life- human perfection up to the highest level, also called as divinisation.

This ancient technique utilises the divine energy for the transformation of human beings, and is called 'transmission' in this system. It is unique in the history of spirituality, and its efficacy in making possible the attainment of the highest ideal of human perfection, or divinisation, in one life, and that too to all and sundry who care to practice it, is something to be wondered at, for the spiritual practice in India was hitherto exclusively the privilege of ascetics who were able to renounce the world.

- Complete Works of Ramachandra, Volume I

Mind over body:

It is of utmost important to not only exercise our body, but also exercise and detoxify our mind. Practices like meditation, pranayama, deep breathing, positive affirmations, maintaining a gratitude journal, are very powerful because they help us find inner balance and peace and handle the stressors of everyday life in a more positive and less damaging way. They promote mind body healing.

- Luke Coutinho, MD, Alternative medicine, from Times of India dated 31 December, '17.

References

1. http://isha.sadhguru.org/blog/yoga-meditation/demystifying-yoga/the-seven-chakras-and-their-significance/

2. http://www.huffingtonpost.com/sadhguru/the-7-chakras-and-their-s_b_844268.html

3. http://www.medindia.net/patients/lifestyleandwellness/seven-chakras-and-our-health.htm

4. http://www.cancer.ca/en/cancer-information/diagnosis-and-treatment/complementary-therapies/music-therapy/?region=on#ixzz4iFkxF9jV

5. http://www.pilu.in/raga-therapy.html

6. https://www.psychologytoday.com/blog/natural-standard/201306/music-therapy-health-and-wellness

Latest developments

'Let everyman count himself immortal. Let him catch the revealation of Jesus in his resurrection. Let him say not merely, 'Christ is rising,' but, 'I shall rise.'

- Phillips Brooks

Cancer has definitely come a long way ever since 2500 BC when it was first recognized by the Egyptian physician Imhotep as a disease for which 'there is no treatment.'

The word 'cancer' originates from the Greek word 'karkinos' meaning crab. Hippocrates, the Greek physician (460-370 B.C) hailed as the father of modern medicine, gave the name to the disease because tumours that are the visible evidence of many types of cancer reminded him of a crab with a central body (the tumour or lump) from which several rays- the legs, spread into the surrounding tissue.

Persian Queen Atossa was diagnosed with breast cancer and underwent the most primitive form of mastectomy performed by her own slave.

New discoveries and advancements in medical science have shown the ability of modern medicines to change the course of the disease and the human capability to fight them successfully. Researchers are closing in on cancer and a breakthrough in finding a cure for the disease may not be far away.

Rise and prevalence of cancer in India

Based on the data between 2010 and 2012, it is predicted that at some point during their lifetime approximately 39.6% of women and men will be diagnosed with cancer. In India it is estimated that 14.5 lakh people are living with the disease, with over 7 lakh new cases being registered every year and 5,56,400 deaths which are said to be cancer related. An estimated 71% of all cancer related deaths are occurring in the age group between 30 to 69 years. With lung, colorectal, pharynx, stomach, head and neck, and lever were the five most common sites of cancer diagnosed among men in 2012; for the same period, the five common sites of cancer diagnosed among women were breast, ovary, lip, and oral cavity, lung and cervix.

Tobacco use is linked to around 20% of global cancer deaths and 70% of global lung cancer. Lung cancer is one of the commonest cancers, accounting for 13% of all new cancer cases and 19% of cancer related deaths worldwide. The increasing prevalence of smoking has resulted in lung cancer reaching epidemic proportions in India, where an estimated 2500 deaths every day can be linked to tobacco-related diseases. In 2010, smoking accounted for an estimated 9,30,000 deaths; 1 in 5 deaths among men and 1 in 20 among women.

The National Cancer Registry puts breast cancer as the most common and cervical cancer as the second most common cancer in women in India. Although the Indian Council of Medical Research reports suggest that cancer of the cervix has become the third most common cancer after breast and lung cancer. It is estimated that for every two women newly diagnosed with breast cancer one dies, while every 8 minutes one woman dies of cervical cancer.

Breast cancer accounts for 27% of all cancers in women in India, with the incidence rising in the early thirties and peaking at ages 50-64 years. It is estimated that 1 in 28 women is likely to develop breast cancer during her lifetime. Cervical cancer accounts for 22.9% of all cancer cases in women. Being the third largest cause of cancer deaths in India, it accounts for nearly 20% of all cancer related deaths. It generally affects the 21 to 67 age group, with the median age of occurrence being 38 years. As compared to the urban women, rural women are at higher risk of developing cervical cancer. Since survival rates improve if the condition is diagnosed and treated early, screening for cervical cancer is important.

(Source: 'World Cancer Day', The Times of India, 4 February, 2017)

Cancer and chances of cure

As per Dr. Ramakant Deshpande of Asian Cancer Institute, those who approach in the first stage of cancer often have 85% chances of cure; in stage 2, there are 60% chances of cure; in stage 3, it falls to 30% and those who start treatment at stage 4 will not survive for more than five years. He further adds that the symptoms in certain types of cancer; if based in publicly knowledgeable areas like pancreas and lungs are easier to detect and these patients approach a doctor at a pre-palpable stage.

But if cancer is not specific, it is often misunderstood to be stomach ailment or cough and is neglected. Such patients consult a doctor in advanced stages.

(Source: The Times of India, dated 06 February, 2017).

Nipping in the bud

Diseases that are diagnosed early on, before they have had the chance to get big or spread, are more likely to be treated successfully.

TV Channel 5 news had a top story highlighting how an alarming number of people who came to the Accident and Emergency wards of hospitals for cuts and bruises, were being diagnosed with suffering from advanced cancer. Many feel that an early diagnosis would lead to a better outcome and, this in essence is correct.

What can be derived from Channel 5 TV's news report is that cancer in UK has the poorest rate of survival when compared with the rest of Europe. The news report also included several stories of patients who complained that their diseases went undiagnosed despite repeated visits to their GP's for symptoms that persisted. Another report had an interview with a GP who said that every tummy pain cannot be deeply investigated for cancer.

Strangely, the state of art or rather the body in this case, is such that any disease does not become evident before being reasonably advanced. This is true of heart diseases, cancers, and many other such conditions. In essence a cancer of the lung is painless unless spread and this is the case with many cancers. In fact when a cancer of the lung is spread and pain makes its appearance from the involvement of the covers of the lungs or surrounding structures, it is already inoperable. Lung cancer is difficult to diagnose as its symptoms only show up in the advanced stages.

To diagnose a cancer of the lung early, one would have to literally perform a scan on the lungs every month. Occasionally, a lucky patient who harbors a tumour, and this has been repeatedly observed in cases of cancer of large bowels that they sometimes bleed with blood thinners given for heart diseases. This is actually a blessing in disguise because cancer is thus diagnosed early.

Early diagnoses of any disease are difficult. And please do not let this be a license for doctors to do a whole load of expensive tests like scans, MRIs, sonograms etc. Early diagnose requires an extremely judicious, clinical judgment regarding when to investigate further in every clinical situation.

(Dr. Altaf Patel, published in Mumbai Mirror dated 23 May, 2017)

Vitamin A in diet can help fight cancer

Intake of Vitamin A in diet could help treat several forms of cancer due to its ability to control the malignant cells, a new study has found.

Scientists have hailed the discovery as a 'new dawn' in cancer treatment after finding a link between malignant cells and lack of Vitamin A.

Experts at the University of York found that cancer cells are under control of a derivative of the Vitamin, known as retinoic acid.

They believe that Vitamin A can be used as new anti-cancer treatment and advised people to ensure they include adequate levels of the nutrient in their diets.

Study was carried out on prostate cancer cells but Professor Norman Maitland of Yorkshire Cancer Research believes the treatment could apply to other cancers as well. Maitland however, warned people not to rush out to buy Vitamin A supplements, which could be toxic and even cancerous in high doses.

Instead he advised people to take Vitamin A in their daily diet, including oily fish, carrots, liver, red pepper and dark leafy vegetables.

Researchers hope that Vitamin A can be used to prevent prostate cancer and that a derivative of Vitamin A could help destroy prostate cancer cells or make them more treatable once they have started to spread.

Retinoic acid is already used to treat blood cancer and has been extremely successful in improving survival rates to 80%. The study is published in the journal 'Nucleic Acids.'

(Source: The Times of India)

Vitamin C can boost fight against brain cancer

Researchers claim to have found evidence that Vitamin C can boost tumour death in brain cancer patients, a finding which could pave the way for an effective treatment for the disease. An International team, led by University of Otago, says research has revealed that high doses of Vitamin C make it easier for radiation therapy to kill brain tumour cells in cancer patients.

In their study, the researchers actually analyzed how combining high dose Vitamin C with radiation affected survival of cancer cells isolated from glioblastoma multiforme (GBM) brain tumours and compared this with survival of normal cells.

The findings revealed that high dose Vitamin C by itself caused DNA damage and cell death which was more pronounced when high dose Vitamin C was given just prior to radiation. Lead author Dr. Patries Herst said GBM patients have a poor prognosis because aggressive GBM tumours are very resistant to radiation therapy.

(Source: The Times of India, Mumbai edition)

Cancer cure likely in 5 to 10 years

An effective cure for all types of cancer could be 5 to 10 years away. Survival rates have increased over the last five decades from 24% the early 1970s to about 50%. Prof. Karol Sikora, former head of WHO's cancer programme, said that advances in genetics meant doctors would soon be able to prescribe drugs specifically targeted at each individual's cancer.

(As reported in The Times of India)

Some encouraging medical advancements

An experimental gene therapy that turns a patient's own blood cells into cancer killers worked in a major study, with more than one-third of very sick lymphoma patients showing no sign of disease six months after a single treatment.

Treatment involves filtering a patient's blood to remove key immune system soldiers called T-cells, altering them in the laboratory to contain a gene that targets cancer, and giving them back intravenously. Doctors call it a 'living drug'- as it permanently altered cells that multiply.

(Source: The Times of India, Mumbai edition dated 01 March, 2017)

Scientists discover new types of white blood cells

Researchers from New York University, Harward University and MIT's Broad Institute, have identified two
new dentritic cell subtypes and two monocyte subtypes. They have also discovered a new dentritic cell progenitor.

Two important white blood cell types in our bodies help defend from infection- dentritic cells and monocytes.

The next step is to find out what each of these cell types does to the body's immune system both when healthy and during diseases.

(Source: The Times of India dated 24 April, 2017)

Nanoparticle that shrinks tumours

Scientists have developed a new-cancer fighting nanoparticle aimed at shrinking breast cancer tumours, at the same time preventing recurrence of the disease.

In a study conducted by the researchers at Mayo Clinic in the USA, mice that received an injection with the nanoparticle showed a 70 to 80% reduction in tumour size.

The mice also showed resistance to tumour recurrence, even when exposed to cancer cells a month later.

The mice treated with these nanoparticles showed a lasting anti-cancer effect.

(Source: The Times of India dated 3 May, 2017)

Bra that can detect cancer

A student from Mexico has designed a bra that can help in the early detection of breast cancer.

The boy was inspired by his mother's battle with the disease.

The bra is equipped with around 200 biosensors, which maps the surface of the breast and also monitors changes in temperature, shape and weight.

The bra shape of the detector helps the breasts to remain in the normal, actual and same position so that the monitoring is carried out in the real condition.

(Source: The Times of India dated 4 May, 2017)

Photodynamic therapy (PDT)

PDT uses medications to make cancer cells and other abnormal cells vulnerable to high-intensity light energy, such as from lasers. It can be used to treat a variety of cancerous and precancerous conditions.

Photodynamic therapy involves applying or infusing a special drug (photosensitizer) that makes the cells light sensitive. For cancers on or near the surface of the skin, the drug may be applied topically. For other cancers, the drug may be infused into a vein.

After the photosensitizer is taken up by the target tissue, the expert exposes the cancer cells to a specific wavelength and energy of light that activates the drug and destroys the cancerous or precancerous cells.

For cancers inside the body, this may require passing the light down a thin, flexible tube and into the esophagus or windpipe (trachea) to reach the area. The light kills the cells that have absorbed the light-sensitive medication.

(http://www.mayoclinic.org/tests-procedures/photodynamic-therapy/home)

Light can trick immune system to attack cancer

Scientists have discovered a simple and practical way to kill cancer cells by using light to steer immune cells to attack the tumours.

Researchers at University of Rochester Medical Centre in US describe their method as similar to 'sending light on a spy mission to track down cancer cells.'

In immunotherapy, instead of directly killing cancer cells, it tells the immune system to act in certain ways by stimulating T cells to attack the disease.

Minsoo Kim, professor at University of Rochester, conducted a study to understand and develop light sensitive molecules that could efficiently guide T-cells towards tumours.

(Source: The Times of India, Mumbai edition dated 16 May, 2017)

Eating nuts may cut risk of colon cancer returning

Colon cancer survivors who ate at least 57 grams of tree nuts a week- roughly 48 almonds or 36 cashews –were significantly less likely to have their cancer return or to die from their cancer than those who did not eat nuts, US researchers from Dena- Farber Cancer Institute in Boston have claimed.

(Source: The Times of India, Mumbai edition dated 20 May, 2017)

Hibiscus leaf could help treat melanoma

A new study in the *Journal of Food Science* found that hibiscus sabdariffa leaf polyphenolic extract (HLP) may induce human melanoma cell death and may serve as a chemotherapeutic agent to eliminate cancer cells without significant harmful effects to normal cells.   (Source: Mumbai Mirror, dated 14 March, 2015)

New designer viruses can help fight cancer: Study

Scientists have created artificial 'designer' viruses that can target cancer by alerting the body's immune system and sending killer cells to fight tumours.

Most cancer cells only provoke a limited reaction by the body's immune system and can thus grow without appreciable resistance. By contrast, viral infections cause the body to release alarm signals, stimulating immune system to use all available means to fight the invader. Researchers at the University of Geneva and the University of Basel in Switzerland have built innovative designer viruses that release alarm signals typical of viral infections. The researchers have integrated certain proteins into the virus that are otherwise found only in cancer cells.

In their study on mice, researchers found that designer viruses enabled the immune system to recognise these cancer proteins as dangerous. The researchers hope that the new findings and technologies will soon be used in cancer treatments and so help to further increase their success rates.

(Source: The Times of India, Mumbai edition dated 30 May, 2017)

Scientists discover how cancer spreads, and the way to slow down metastasis

In the ongoing war against cancer; an international team led by scientists from Johns Hopkins University has, for the first time, found what causes the spread of cancer and what could slow it down.

This is important because 90% of cancer deaths are caused when cancer cells break off from the origin and start spreading elsewhere in the body. There are no existing drugs to stop this spread, known as metastasis, of cancer.

The researchers found that when cells get densely packed they secrete two proteins that deliver a stark message to the cells - go away. This causes the cancer cells to break off from the pack and float through the blood stream or lymphatic system to other sites and start growing afresh. It's like waiting for a table in a severely overcrowded restaurant and then getting a message that says you need to take your appetite elsewhere. The study has been published in Nature Communications.

The researchers have found that it was not the overall size of a primary tumour that caused cancer cells to spread, but how tightly those cells are jammed together when they break away from the tumour.

The researchers have found a medication mix that kept this microscopic message from being delivered. The team cautioned that this treatment had been tested in animals but not yet on humans.

Nevertheless, it said the discovery contributes to a promising new focus for cancer research; disrupting the biochemical activity that prods cancer cells to spread through the body.

(Source: The Times of India, Mumbai edition dated 31 May, 2017)

Two drugs raise hopes for ovarian, breast cancer patients

One of the study's senior authors, Denis Wirtz, from the Johns Hopkins and director of its Physical Sciences Oncology Center; said no commercial drugs are now being produced specifically to inhibit metastasis because drug companies believe the best way to stop cancer from spreading is to destroy the primary tumour.

Pharmaceutical companies view metastasis as a by product of tumour growth. The study conducted by the researchers looked more closely at the steps that actually initiate metastasis. This treatment has potential to inhibit metastasis and improve cancer patient outcomes.

The team found that two existing drugs- Tocilizumab and Reparaxin – prevented cancer cells from getting their marching orders. Tocilizumab is an approved medication for rheumatoid arthritis and is in trials for use in ovarian cancer cases. Reparaxin is being evaluated as a possible treatment for breast cancer.

During the experiment when these drugs were used together, growth of primary tumour was not stopped but spread of cancer cells decreased significantly. The researchers have discovered a new signalling pathway that, when blocked, could potentially curb cancer's ability to metastasis. (The Times of India, Mumbai edition dated 31 July, 2017)

Yoga can make cancer patients sleep better:

Yoga can dramatically boost the wellbeing of cancer patients, research reveals. New studies presented at the world's largest cancer conference found just four weeks of practicing yoga, including gentle hatha yoga can improve wellbeing and reduce tiredness. It is found that yoga significantly improved both fatigue and sleep quality.

Yoga could help alleviate some of the very difficult side-effects following breast cancer treatment, such as fatigue and sleep deprivation.

- Mumbai Mirror dated 10 June, 2017.

From my experiences in music and meditation, which I began many years ago, I know that we have another side to us, a big spirit that is in all of us, that tells you that you're part of the universe and it is part of you. This knowledge is life-changing but we can only have it if we go in search for it. All the work one does in meditation is so that you can hack your way through the superficial and ridiculous thoughts that invade us constantly. We are extremely mysterious nd full of magic.

- British jazz-fusion guitar maestro John McLaughlin.

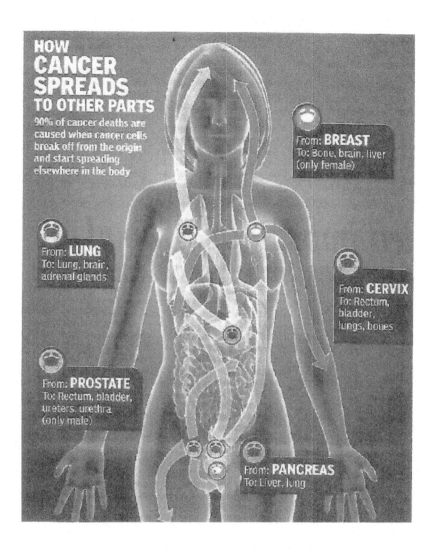

We have met the future and it is food. Our cures are mostly inside us. What we do to our bodies determines pretty much what our bodies will do to us. The future of cancer prevention, then, seems to me very bright indeed.

We have also become more aware of the mechanisms of cancer. There was a time not so very far distant when no one had a really clear idea of what provoked malignant cell changes, much less what could be done to prevent them, but much has changed.

You can alter the activation or inactivation by your genes by the food you eat. Science has discovered that the body contains tumour-producing genes (oncogenes) and also tumour-suppression genes. Moreover, there are substances in the body-such as the cycloxygenase-2 (COX-2) enzyme that turn these genes on and off.

In the years to come, we are going to learn a tremendous amount about these genes, and that will make a difference to cancer prevention that is impossible to overestimate. We already know so much about the foods and phytonutrients that protect us, however, that we can probably secure a cancer-free future for ourselves and our families now.

- From the book-'Lower your cancer risk now!'

World Cancer day is celebrated every year on February 4.

Prayer

Narayaneeyam is a condensed version of the Bhagavata Purana (18,000 verses). It condenses the entire Bhagavata Purana into 1034 verses, divided into 100 dasakams or cantos.

Narayaneeyam was composed by Melpathur Narayana Bhattathiri (1560-1666 AD). It is said that the work has the blessings of Guruvayoorappan or Lord Krishna, the presiding diety of Guruvayur.

The sloka given below from Narayaneeyam (Dasakam 8, Sloka 13) is a very powerful sloka that has been recommended by the most revered Sankaracharya of Kanchipuram Shree Chandrasekharendra Saraswathy Swami for curing cancer and other chronic ailments.

अस्मिन् परात्मन् ननु पाद्मकल्पे
त्वमित्थमुत्थापतिपद्मयोनि: ।
अनन्तभूमा मम रोगराशि
निरुन्धि वातालयवास विष्णो ॥

Asmin paraathman nanu paadmakalpe
Thvamithamutthaapitha padmayonihi I
Anantha bhoomaa mama roga raashim,
Nirundhi vaathaalaya vaasa vishno.

About the author

 C K Sreedharan is presently working as Assistant Professor in Pillai Institute of Management Studies & Research, New Panvel, Navi Mumbai, State of Maharashtra, India.

C K Sreedharan is a mechanical engineer from Delhi College of Engineering, Delhi University. He also holds MBA in International Business, MBA in Banking & Finance, and Diploma in Training & Development from ISTD, New Delhi and PhD in management.

He is a certified lead assessor for ISO: 9001, ISO: 14001 and OHSAS: 18001. He is an accredited energy manager and energy auditor of Bureau of Energy Efficiency, New Delhi. He is also a certified Six Sigma Black belt.

He is a Reiki Grandmaster.

C K Sreedharan has more than 27 years of industrial experience and has more than 15 years of teaching experience. He has authored a book on 'International Business' for post graduate management stream and has published and presented several research papers in national and international journals and conferences.

He was also a technical and system consultant for several government, semi-government and private sector organizations. He was a panel auditor for Det Norske Veritas, a reputed international third party certification agency.

He was diagnosed with multiple myeloma, a type of blood cancer in April 2008. After surviving the dreaded cancer, he has developed a passion for writing.

Battle Against Multiple Myeloma- A true story by the cancer survivor- is an attempt by the author to share his real life trauma and his own personal experience in battling with the dreaded disease. In this book, the author covers all aspects of the disease right from detection to treatment.

A distinguishing feature of this book is the sharing of actual medical and laboratory reports of the author, which helps in clear understanding. Author also provides extensive information on cancer prevention and ways to strengthen the immune system of the body. Immune system is the body's own powerful self defense mechanism, which protects the body against all diseases, including cancer.

This book has helped many cancer victims worldwide.

Wind Beneath the Wings- A Story of Love, Passion and Romance- is a romantic and a passionate love story.

Vivek is a multifaceted genius and evolves into a successful engineer. His past struggles have given him tenacity and strong self belief. He is charismatic, leads by example and becomes a role model for others. He transforms an ordinary organization into a world class organization through his ingenuity.

Charulatha, the dynamic and beautiful director of the company where Vivek works as the Works Manager, is strongly attracted towards Vivek and develops a strong fascination for him. Sandhya, Vivek's childhood sweetheart is waiting on her wings to marry Vivek.

Both the women are extraordinary, strong- willed, self- respecting and women of substance. Vivek is passionately attracted towards one woman, and his sense of gratitude forces him to drift towards the other woman.

Who will propel Vivek as an invisible force to achieve greater success in life as wind beneath his powerful wings? To know, read the interesting romantic novel.

Overcome cancer through lifestyle reorientation – Discusses about various ways through which lifestyle can be reoriented to overcome and challenge the disease.

In India there are many well researched and highly effective natural ways of treating our body through herbs, food, yoga, meditation and other practices which are in tune and harmony with the nature as well as with the human body.

There are foods and herbs that can strengthen immune system, our body's powerful self-defence mechanism against any disease, including cancer.

This book also provides alternate approaches to cancer management and prevention. This book has inspired and motivated not only the cancer patients but others as well.

The Bonded Tribal- An organic love story –

Surya is a tribal and his family is trapped in the dreaded bonded labour system. Surya's father rebels against the system for which the family faces the wrath of the powerful landlords.

A young Surya retaliates by murdering the landlords. After serving his sentence in a reform home, Surya develops passion for organic farming and actively works for tribal empowerment.

Surya's deep scar on his face scares many, but not the damsel Dr. Sanjana. The chance meeting and the subsequent unexpected interactions result in blossoming of love between Surya and Sanjana.

Dr. Gautam, a cosmetic plastic surgeon, is also attracted by Sanjana and is determined to marry her. Gautam is known for his expertise on body shaping of women and making them celebrities in the glamour industry. Gautam is believed to have enjoyed cosy sexual relationship with many of his celebrity clients.

Sanjana yearns to marry Surya but her family favours Gautam.

How this intriguing triangular love story will unfold? Read the gripping love story of- The Bonded Tribal- An organic love story.

All the above books are self-published through Kindle platform and are available in electronic as well as paperback versions at *www.amazon.com.*

To know more about C K Sreedharan email at *cksiyengar@gmail.com* or visit www.sreedharanck.com or www.amazon/author/sreedharanck.

******

Made in the USA
Coppell, TX
24 September 2021